INITIAL STEPS IN REBUILDING THE HEALTH SECTOR IN EAST TIMOR

Jim Tulloch, Fadia Saadah, Rui Maria de Araujo,
Rui Paulo de Jesus, Sergio Lobo, Isabel Hemming,
Jane Nassim, and Ian Morris

Roundtable on the Demography of Forced Migration
Committee on Population

NATIONAL RESEARCH COUNCIL
OF THE NATIONAL ACADEMIES

and
Program on Forced Migration and Health at the
Mailman School of Public Health
Columbia University

THE NATIONAL A
Washing
www.n~p.~~~

D1211137

THE NATIONAL ACADEMIES PRESS   500 Fifth Street, N.W.   Washington, DC 20001

NOTICE: The project that is the subject of this report was approved by the Governing Board of the National Research Council, whose members are drawn from the councils of the National Academy of Sciences, the National Academy of Engineering, and the Institute of Medicine. The members of the committee responsible for the report were chosen for their special competences and with regard for appropriate balance.

This study was supported by a grant to the National Academy of Sciences and the Mailman School of Public Health of Columbia University by the Andrew W. Mellon Foundation. Any opinions, findings, conclusions, or recommendations expressed in this publication are those of the authors and do not necessarily reflect the view of the organizations or agencies that provided support for this project.

International Standard Book Number 0-309-08901-8 (Book)
International Standard Book Number 0-309-50584-4 (PDF)

Additional copies of this report are available from the National Academies Press, 500 Fifth Street, N.W., Lockbox 285, Washington, DC 20055; (800) 624-6242 or (202) 334-3313 (in the Washington metropolitan area); Internet, http://www.nap.edu

Printed in the United States of America

Suggested citation: National Research Council. (2003). *Initial Steps in Rebuilding the Health Sector in East Timor.* Jim Tulloch, Fadia Saadah, Rui Maria de Araujo, Rui Paulo de Jesus, Sergio Lobo, Isabel Hemming, Jane Nassim, and Ian Morris. Roundtable on the Demography of Forced Migration. Committee on Population, Division of Behavioral and Social Sciences and Education and Program on Forced Migration and Health at the Mailman School of Public Health of Columbia University. Washington, DC: The National Academies Press.

ROUNDTABLE ON THE DEMOGRAPHY OF FORCED MIGRATION
2003

CHARLES B. KEELY *(Chair)*, Walsh School of Foreign Service, Georgetown University

LINDA BARTLETT, Division of Reproductive Health, Centers for Disease Control and Prevention, Atlanta

RICHARD BLACK, Center for Development and Environment, University of Sussex

STEPHEN CASTLES, Refugee Studies Centre, University of Oxford

WILLIAM GARVELINK, Bureau of Humanitarian Response, U.S. Agency for International Development, Washington, DC

ANDRE GRIEKSPOOR, Emergency and Humanitarian Action Department, World Health Organization, Geneva

JOHN HAMMOCK, Feinstein International Famine Center, Tufts University

BELA HOVY, Program Coordination Section, United Nations High Commissioner for Refugees, Geneva

JENNIFER LEANING, School of Public Health, Harvard University

DOMINIQUE LEGROS, Epi Centre, Médecins Sans Frontières, Paris

NANCY LINDBORG, Mercy Corps, Washington, DC

CAROLYN MAKINSON, The Andrew W. Mellon Foundation, New York

SUSAN F. MARTIN, Institute for the Study of International Migration, Georgetown University

W. COURTLAND ROBINSON, Center for Refugee and Disaster Studies, Johns Hopkins University

SHARON STANTON RUSSELL, Center for International Studies, Massachusetts Institute of Technology

WILLIAM SELTZER, Department of Sociology and Anthropology, Fordham University

PAUL SPIEGEL, International Emergency and Refugee Health Branch, Centers for Disease Control and Prevention, Atlanta

RONALD WALDMAN, Mailman School of Public Health, Columbia University

ANTHONY ZWI, School of Public Health and Community Medicine, University of New South Wales

HOLLY REED, *Program Officer*

Preface

In response to the need for more research on displaced persons, the Committee on Population developed the Roundtable on the Demography of Forced Migration in 1999. This activity, which is supported by the Andrew W. Mellon Foundation, provides a forum in which a diverse group of experts can discuss the state of knowledge about demographic structures and processes among people who are displaced by war and political violence, famine, natural disasters, or government projects or programs that destroy their homes and communities. The roundtable includes representatives from operational agencies, with long-standing field and administrative experience. It includes researchers and scientists with both applied and scholarly expertise in medicine, demography, and epidemiology. The group also includes representatives from government, international organizations, donors, universities, and nongovernmental organizations.

The roundtable is organized to be as inclusive as possible of relevant expertise and to provide occasions for substantive sharing to increase knowledge for all participants, with a view toward developing cumulative facts to inform policy and programs in complex humanitarian emergencies. To this aim, the roundtable has held annual workshops on a variety of topics, including mortality patterns in complex emergencies, demographic assessment techniques in emergency settings, and research ethics among conflict-affected and displaced populations.

Another role for the roundtable is to serve as a promoter of the best research in the field. The field is rich in practitioners but is lacking a coherent body of research. In recent years a number of attempts to codify health policies and practices for the benefit of the humanitarian assistance community have been launched. The SPHERE Project—a group of nongovernmental organizations—has produced a set of guidelines for public health interventions in emergency settings. The nongovernmental organization Médecins Sans Frontières has published a manual entitled *Refugee Health: An Approach to Emergency Situations* (1997). In addition, a number of short-term training courses have been developed, including the Health Emergencies in Large Populations (HELP) course sanctioned by the International Committee of the Red Cross and the Public Health in Complex Emergencies course, which is partially funded by the U.S. Agency for International Development. All of these are intended to convey the state of the art to health care practitioners who serve refugees.

Yet the scientific basis for these currently recommended best practices is rarely presented along with the guidelines. And many of the current recommendations are based on older, perhaps even outdated, analyses and summaries of the literature. Furthermore, even when data are available, they are frequently inconsistent, unreliable, and spotty. Few of the currently recommended practices are based on scientifically valid epidemiological or clinical studies conducted among the refugee populations they are intended to benefit. Recognition of the need for a more evidence-based body of knowledge to guide the public health work practiced by the relief community has led to a widespread call for more epidemiological research. This was acted on by the World Health Organization, which formed an Advisory Group for Research in Emergency Settings.

In some sense the current wave of recommendations represents the end of a cycle of learning that began with the publication of a series of papers in the medical literature in the late 1980s. The data contained in those papers were originally generated during the period 1978–1986. But the world and the nature of forced migration have changed a great deal since then, and the relevance of those data can now be called into question. Therefore, the roundtable and the Program on Forced Migration and Health at the Mailman School of Public Health of Columbia University have commissioned a series of epidemiological reviews and case studies on priority public health problems for forced migrants that will update the state of knowledge. These occasional monographs are individually authored documents presented to the roundtable and any recommendations or conclusions are solely attributable to the authors. It is hoped these reports will result in the formulation of newer and more scientifically sound public health practices and policies and will identify areas in which new research is needed to guide the development of health care policy. Many of the monographs may represent newer areas of concern for which no summary information is available in the published literature.

The present monograph—on rebuilding the health sector in East Timor following the nation's struggle for independence—is the second in this series. It provides an overview of the state of the health system before, during, and after reconstruction and discusses achievements and failures in the rebuilding process, using an informative case study to draw conclusions for potential improvements to the process in other post-conflict settings. Other topics under consideration in the series include reviews of current knowledge on psychosocial issues, reproductive health, malnutrition, and diarrheal diseases, as well as other case studies.

This monograph has been reviewed by individuals chosen for their diverse perspectives and technical expertise in accordance with procedures approved by the National Research Council's Report Review Committee. The purpose of this independent review was to provide candid and critical comments that would assist the institution in making the published mono-graph as accurate and as sound as possible. The review comments and draft manuscript remain confidential.

Charles B. Keely of Georgetown University served as review coor-dinator for this monograph. We wish to thank the following individuals for their participation in the review of this report: Dennis Dijkzeul, The Institute for International Law of Peace and Armed Conflict, Ruhr Universität Bochum, and Sharon Stanton Russell, Massachusetts Institute of Technology.

Although the individuals listed above provided constructive comments and suggestions, it must be emphasized that responsibility for this mono-graph rests entirely with the authors.

We would also like to acknowledge Egbert Sondorp, Health Policy Unit, London School of Hygiene and Tropical Medicine, and Anthony Zwi, School of Public Health and Community Medicine, University of New South Wales, who took the time to look over and suggest improve-ments to Appendix C.

This series of monographs is being made possible by a special collabo-ration between the Roundtable on the Demography of Forced Migration of The National Academies and the Program on Forced Migration and Health at the Mailman School of Public Health of Columbia University. We thank the Andrew W. Mellon Foundation for its continued support of the work of the roundtable and the program at Columbia. A special thanks is due Carolyn Makinson of the Mellon Foundation for her enthusiasm and significant expertise in the field of forced migration, which she has shared with the roundtable, and for her help in facilitating partnerships such as this.

Most of all, we are grateful to the authors of this report. We hope that this publication contributes to both better policy and better practice in the field.

Charles B. Keely
Chair, Roundtable on the Demography of Forced Migration

Ronald J. Waldman
Member, Roundtable on the Demography of Forced Migration

Holly E. Reed
Program Officer, Roundtable on the Demography of Forced Migration

Contents

Appendixes

Initial Steps in Rebuilding the Health Sector in East Timor

OVERVIEW

In May 2002 Timor Leste (East Timor) emerged as a new nation after centuries of foreign rule and decades of struggle for independence. Its birth was a painful one; a United Nations-brokered Popular Consultation in August 1999, in which an overwhelming majority of the people opted for independence, was followed by several weeks of vengeful violence, looting, and destruction by pro-Indonesia militias. It left the territory and all of its essential services devastated. In this context, the United Nations Transitional Administration in East Timor (UNTAET), with the country's leaders and people and many other partners, set about restoring order and services, building a government structure, and preparing for independence.

This paper summarizes the rehabilitation and development of the health sector from early 2000 to the end of 2001. The health situation in East Timor at the beginning of that period was similar to that of many less developed countries, but it was compounded by several years of deterioration in health services and also by the destruction of late 1999. The situation was characterized by high child and maternal mortality rates and a high prevalence of communicable diseases, including malaria and tuberculosis. The health infrastructure was in total disarray, with more than a third of health facilities totally destroyed and much of the rest substantially damaged. Most equipment and supplies had been looted or damaged beyond use. More than 80 percent of medically qualified staff had returned to Indonesia, and the central health administration was defunct.

Following the period of conflict, the East Timorese health staff did their best to reorganize and provide services, and the international community responded quickly to the need. In particular, international emergency relief nongovernmental organizations (NGOs) moved in to provide health services at many points across the country. Facilitated by the existence of an East Timorese Health Professionals Working Group, UNTAET established the Interim Health Authority (IHA) in February 2000. This body brought together remaining senior East Timorese health staff with the UNTAET health staff to coordinate rehabilitation and development of the sector. The IHA evolved into the Division of Health Services (DHS) in the first transitional government in July 2000 and into the Ministry of Health (MOH) in the second transitional government in September 2001.

In April 2000 a joint donor mission led by the World Bank and the IHA designed the first phase of the Health Sector Rehabilitation and Development Program (HSRDP), which provided the framework for a sectorwide approach to the planning and implementation of activities in the health sector. HSRDP I had two main components: restoring access to basic services for the entire population and development of the health policy and system for the future. A major feature of the program was the development, with NGO partners, of district health plans covering all districts. The second phase of the program was initiated in mid-2001. HSRDP II comprised three components: support to ongoing services, improvement in the scope and quality of services and support systems, and development of policy, regulations, and administrative systems. In both phases a substantial part of the funding came through the multidonor Trust Fund for East Timor (TFET), administered by the World Bank. Recurrent costs were covered through funds administered by UNTAET, and substantial additional support was provided through continued humanitarian assistance and from bilateral development assistance.

Achievements by November 2001 included the establishment and staffing of the government health service across the whole country, including district health management teams in all districts. Drug supplies were reasonably well secured and based on an approved essential drug list. The civil works program was under way for the construction of health centers and a central medical store, and a consultancy was initiated to develop an autonomous medical supply system. Basic services had been restored to most facilities included in the district health plans with the active collaboration of designated NGO partners. Program activities had been initiated on immunization, tuberculosis, HIV/AIDS, malaria, integrated management of childhood illness, mental health, and dental health. The main referral hospital had been handed over to East Timorese management.

To achieve this progress, many constraints had to be overcome, and progress was slow in a number of areas. Policy development proved difficult to get started, especially the adequate involvement of stakeholders, and a long-term plan for human resource development was still lacking at the end of 2001. Staff recruitment was extremely slow, a situation that had consequences for morale and for the credibility of the administration. Procurement of goods, supplies, and consultant services was also slower than expected, often bogged down by the procedural complexities and their interinstitutional differences, and the civil works program was well behind schedule.

Among the challenges faced by those coordinating health sector development were competing objectives and expectations held by the political leaders, the administration, the donors, and other stakeholders. Trying to address incompatible demands and justify directions taken was a drain on limited staff capacity.

Many stakeholders played a role in the reconstruction of the health sector, including the United Nations (UN) agencies, in particular the World Health Organization (WHO), UNICEF, and the United Nations Fund for Population Activities (UNFPA). This paper addresses the authors' perceptions of strengths and weaknesses of only three of the main actors: UNTAET, the World Bank, and the international NGOs. Each contributed very substantially, and each brought constraints, without which progress could perhaps have been much faster.

Paradoxically, the availability of quite considerable financial resources in the first two years of reconstruction may not have been entirely positive. Funding in excess of absorptive capacity and pressure to spend can lead to approaches that will ultimately be unsustainable.

The paper concludes with the authors' thoughts on what could be different in a similar situation in the future. It makes some general recommendations and specific suggestions directed at UN transitional administrations, the World Bank, international NGOs, and those who provide funding. Box 1 is a list of acronyms and abbreviations used in this paper.

BOX 1 Acronyms and Abbreviations

AFAP   Australian Foundation for the Peoples of Asia
ASP   Associacao Saude em Portuguese
AusAID   Australian Agency for International Development

CHA   central health authority (IHA, DHS, or MOH)
CHC   community health center
CIC   Cooperaçao Intercambio e Cultura
CNRM   National Council of the Maubere Resistance
CNRT   National Council of Timorese Resistance

DHP   district health plan
DHS   Division of Health Services
DOTS   directly observed treatment strategy
DPKO   Department of Peace Keeping Operations

ECHO   European Commission Humanitarian Office
EPI   Expanded Programme of Immunization
ETHPWG East Timor Health Professionals Working Group
ETTA   East Timor Transitional Administration

FALINTIL National Liberation Army of East Timor
FRETILIN Revolutionary Front of Independent East Timor

HP   health plan
HSP   health service provider
HSRDP   Health Sector Rehabilitation and Development
           Program

INTRODUCTION

On May 20, 2002 East Timor became independent, the first new country of the 21st century. For more than 400 years this territory had been under the domination of foreign rule, first as a Portuguese colony, then during 24 years of Indonesian occupation.

After the Popular Consultation on the future status of East Timor, organized under the auspices of the United Nations in August 1999, in which autonomy within Indonesia was rejected by the East Timorese people in favor of independence, the territory suffered several weeks of terror and

IMCI	integrated management of childhood illness
IHA	Interim Health Authority
INTERFET	International Force in East Timor
ICRC	International Committee of the Red Cross
IOs	international organizations
MBBS	Bachelor of Medicine and Bachelor of Surgery
MOH	Ministry of Health
MPH	Master of Public Health
NGO	nongovernmental organization
PMU	program management unit
RH	reproductive health
SWAP	sector-wide approach
TA	technical assistance
TFET	Trust Fund for East Timor
UDC	Christian Democratic Union of Timor
UNAMET	United Nations Mission in East Timor
UNFPA	United Nations Fund for Population Activities
UNICEF	United Nations Childrens Fund
UNTAET	United Nations Transitional Administration in East Timor
WHO	World Health Organization
4WD	four-wheel drive

destruction at the hands of pro-Indonesian militia groups backed by uncontrolled elements of the Indonesian army. An apparent scorched earth policy was implemented with terrible efficiency in the few weeks between the referendum and the arrival of the multinational peacekeeping force known as INTERFET. The devastation of the territory, including its infrastructure and public systems, was almost total. At the start of 2000, government services of all types were in ruins; there was no public transportation, no banking system, and few commercial outlets for any type of product. The United Nations, in the form of the UNTAET, formally took on the administration of the territory, including the deployment of UN peace-keeping forces, and was establishing a civilian administration covering all sectors. It is in this context that efforts were started to reconstruct a health system for East Timor.

In post-conflict situations, the rush of external assistance to alleviate suffering and or prevent further disaster almost inevitably leads to major challenges of coordinating and rationalizing the response. East Timor is one of the more recent cases. This report attempts to briefly describe the process of rehabilitation and development of the health system during 2000–2001, including some of the achievements, the constraints that were faced, and the roles of some of the main actors. It does not pretend to be an academic treatment of the topic of health in post-conflict situations and does not make reference to earlier work in this area. Many of the observations made here may have already been recorded in other settings.

The report comments on the development of the health sector during 2000 and 2001 from the perspective of those trying to implement the reha-bilitation and development program. Although significant advances were made in a short period of time, the process was at times frustrating and inefficient. The authors were well placed to observe the failings and defi-ciencies of the effort in East Timor from the inside.[1] In our view, most of the numerous institutions and individuals involved acted in good faith and with commitment to the cause. Much of the inefficiency observed we judged to be due to the inflexibility of institutional systems. We do not view this as inevitable and hope that this paper can stimulate discussion of changes that could be made to respond more effectively to future post-conflict situations. If this paper is critical of the entities involved, the only intention is to provide a basis for reflection in case the international com-munity is confronted with a similar task in the future. It aims to provide some insights for the various agencies involved into how the process came together at the implementation level and what might be improved in a future rebuilding program in similar circumstances.

---

[1]The authors include the three most senior East Timorese officials of the central health authority during 2000 and 2001, the two most senior members of the UNTAET health sector team, one of whom also served as the director of the program management unit of the part of the HSRDP funded through the multidonor TFET administered by the World Bank, and the three World Bank, Washington, staff most directly involved in the HSRDP, includ-ing the two task managers who served in succession in that role.

Appendix A contains a brief chronology of major events in the political development and establishment of government in East Timor as well as selected developments in the health sector. A useful summary of the situation in 2000 can be found in United Nations (2000).

THE HEALTH CONTEXT

The population of East Timor varied during 2000–2001 with the progressive return of those who had fled to West Timor during this time. The population was between 750,000 and 800,000, with approximately one-third in the capital, Dili, and the larger towns, and the remainder scattered in small rural villages and hamlets, many inaccessible by road. The rural population is mainly engaged in subsistence agriculture. During 2000–2001 the difficulties of subsistence were increased by the aftermath of the destruction and looting, during the events of 1999, of entire hamlets, along with cereal and seed reserves and the slaughter of livestock.

The main health problems of the population of East Timor are like those of many developing countries with similar climatic conditions and level of development. The main causes of death in 1997–1998 were reported as pneumonia and diarrhea in children; malaria is highly endemic, and the prevalence of tuberculosis extremely high. Reproductive health problems also contribute much to the ill health of the population.

Although few reliable and current data were available, it was estimated, based on pre-1999 reports, the precarious living conditions, and the deterioration of health services, that the infant mortality rate in 2000 was around 125 deaths per 1,000 live births or higher and the mortality rate under age 5 was 200 or higher. Reported figures suggest that the maternal mortality rate was in the range of 550–900 deaths per 100,000. Whatever the exact figures, East Timor in 2000 had a health profile similar to some of the poorest developing countries despite the previous relatively large number of health facilities and staff.

The Health System After September 1999

A survey conducted in January 2000 put some shocking numbers on the known extensive destruction of the health infrastructure. It found that 35 percent of all health facilities had been totally destroyed. Only 23 percent of buildings had escaped without major damage, including, fortuitously, the referral hospitals in Dili and the district of Baucau. Virtually all equipment and supplies had been looted or damaged beyond use. Most doctors and senior health management staff had left, returning to Indonesia. Only around 25 East Timorese doctors and one specialist remained. The central administration of the health system was completely destroyed.

In the months immediately following the conflict, both national and international groups moved quickly to deliver health services. Many of the remaining senior East Timorese health professionals organized themselves to form the East Timor Health Professionals Working Group (ETHPWG). With some external input from the World Health Organization and others, by December ETHPWG had developed a rough plan for future health services. International NGOs had moved in quickly and were providing emergency services. Although some services were being provided across much of the territory, coverage was uneven. A Joint Health Working Group, consisting of members of the ETHPWG, the UN agencies concerned with health, and the NGOs, did its best to coordinate activities among its members and with UNTAET, but the focus, appropriately, was on emergency relief rather than on planning how to rebuild the system.

Establishment of "Government" Coordination

On February 16, 2000, UNTAET created the Interim Health Authority, consisting of 16 senior East Timorese health professionals at the central level (plus 1 in each of 13 districts) and the 6 UNTAET health staff who had by that time arrived in East Timor. One East Timorese health specialist and one UNTAET staff member coordinated the group. Its physical resources consisted of one vehicle and a few tables and chairs. The lack of vehicles was to become a major constraint. The authors believe that the health sector was consistently neglected in the distribution of UN vehicles despite the priority verbally given to the sector. Holding meetings of the newly formed IHA was always a challenge, as the "office" of the IHA was in a huge auditorium shared with many other sectors of the transitional administration. Chairs were in short supply, and the noise level at times so high that communication during meetings was close to impossible.

Within a few days, the IHA had formed nine working groups to address what were perceived to be the most pressing issues. The IHA decided that the sooner a development perspective was adopted, the faster a sustainable system could be built. Despite this perspective, it proved difficult for the IHA to avoid spending much of its time and effort reacting to crises and to external offers of support or demands for action or information. The offers and demands, mostly very well intentioned, ranged from being well informed and potentially helpful to being naïve and time wasting. At times the primary motivation appeared to be identifying a niche for a particular organization, often with minimal funding, that had sent someone on an exploratory mission. Even offers accompanied by assurances of long-term support were at times more of a distraction than a help. At one point, for example, in the early weeks of the IHA, three different groups were seeking its endorsement for their plans to rebuild the dental health services. None had the resources or, arguably, the expertise for this task. Similarly, relatively large amounts of the available public health expertise were diverted into dealing with asbestos in destroyed buildings at a time of much more urgent health issues, because of the strong advocacy efforts of one small group. Accusations of unethical neglect of what the group perceived to be a priority public health issue were persistently leveled with very little appreciation of its relative importance.

One of the important early activities of the newly formed IHA was team visits to all of the districts to gather information to inform the upcoming first Joint Donor Health Mission. This was intended not only to provide a basis for analysis and planning, but also to demonstrate to the donors that the IHA was the authority with the best information and the institution "in charge" of the situation in the health sector. Despite the inevitable limitations of the information collected, this proved to be important in establishing the IHA's credibility.

HEALTH SECTOR REHABILITATION AND DEVELOPMENT PROGRAM

Phase I

In March–April 2000, the first Joint Donor Mission for the planning of the rehabilitation of the health sector took place. It was led jointly by the World Bank and the IHA. Members of the mission included representatives of the governments of Australia and Portugal and of the European Commission. The team, encompassing a wide range of technical expertise, prepared a framework for action that became the HSRDP. It was considered from the outset that a sector-wide approach was critical to provide overall guidance to all activities in the health sector. This proved to be fundamental to the excellent cooperation among all major actors in the health sector over the ensuing two years. The HSRDP had two main components: restoring access to basic services for the entire population and development of the health policy and system for the future. The HSRDP was the basis for a World Bank grant to the health sector supported by $12.7 million (US) from the multidonor TFET over 15 months. The project supported by this grant was prepared, appraised, and negotiated within six weeks, demonstrating the commitment of the World Bank to streamline its usual procedures in light of the special situation in East Timor. However, it took UNTAET an additional 10 weeks to agree to and meet the conditions for effectiveness of the grant, a vital loss of time. This delay was due to a number of factors, including issues around central control versus delegated authority, the legal aspects of this and other arrangements, and the slow identification and approval of essential staff for the project's management unit. More generally, the delay was due to overload of the few competent staff empowered to make decisions, the inefficiency of a system making up procedures as it went along, and, in the authors' view, a legal and administrative approach that was unduly cautious given the urgency of the situation.

In the implementation of the first component, a critical element of the transitional strategy was reaching agreement with NGOs to work with the IHA to prepare district health plans. Despite initial reluctance by some of the international NGOs to be coordinated by the "government," that is, UNTAET, the legitimate role of the IHA was eventually accepted and a close relationship with the NGOs ensued. This allowed rationalization of the distribution of the resources by requesting one or sometimes two NGOs to take the lead in each district based on an approved plan.

Table 1 shows the distribution of the main international NGOs providing health services in the districts, outside of the Dili (capital) district, before and after the development of district health plans. The collaboration of the NGOs allowed for the simultaneous preparation of district health plans for each of the 12 districts outside Dili, a task beyond the capacity of the IHA alone. In the negotiation of agreements on the district health plans, the IHA did not have the capacity to review them in detail. It therefore placed its emphasis on reviewing, and intentionally limiting, the number of fixed facilities and the numbers of health staff, international and, especially, national. Achievement of good population access was sought through planning the initial use of mobile clinics (nurses with motorcycles) in some areas. These emphases were driven by a strong need to secure the sustainability of the future health system by ensuring that the previous system was not simply put back in place. The system under Indonesian rule

TABLE 1   International NGOs Providing Basic Health Services in East Timor (Excluding Dili District)

District	NGO	
	As of 19 March 2000	As of 30 April 2001, following District Health Plans
Aileu	• OIKOS • World Vision International	• OIKOS • World Vision International
Ainaro	• Timor Aid • CIC/ASP • ICRC	• Timor Aid/AFAP • CIC/ASP
Baucau	• Médecins Sans Frontières, Belgium • German Doctors for Development	• Médecins Sans Frontières, Belgium
Bobonaro	• Médecins Sans Frontières, Holland • World Vision International • Timor Aid • Jesuit Relief Services	• Health Net International
Ermera	• Assistencia Medica International, Portugal • Services for the Health in Asian and African Regions • International Committee of the Red Cross	• Assistencia Medica International, Portugal
Lautem	• Médecins du Monde, Portugal • Alliance of Friends for Medical Care in East Timor • Jesuit Relief Services	• Médecins du Monde, Portugal
Liquiça	• Médecins Sans Frontières, Holland	• Health Net International
Manatuto	• Asistencia Medica International Portugal • Médecins Sans Frontières, France	• Instituto Marques Valle de Flor
Oecussi	• International Medical Corps	• International Medical Corps
Same	• OIKOS	• OIKOS
Suai	• Médecins du Monde, France	• Médecins du Monde, France
Viqueque	• Médecins du Monde, France	• Comite d'Action Medicale

had been characterized by a large number of often overstaffed facilities that were underfunded and underutilized.

An agreement with each NGO was covered by a negotiated memorandum of understanding (see Appendix B). The close collaboration with the NGOs was greatly facilitated by—indeed would not have been possible without—the full collaboration of the European Commission Humanitarian Office (ECHO), which was the major funding source of many of the important NGOs. ECHO agreed to use the district health plans as the basis for funding and also agreed with the IHA on ceilings for selected items, like directly hired staff, rehabilitation, and drugs (the latter by that time being provided in large part by the government). Without such ceilings it would have been difficult for the IHA to limit unwanted effects on the health system arising, for example, from rehabilitation of health facilities in inappropriate sites. The ceilings were, however, sufficiently high to allow basic repairs and initial rehabilitation to all facilities included in the district health plans.

Not surprisingly, the planned downsizing of the health system provoked some strong reaction from some NGOs and especially from the health workers, already justifiably insecure about their futures, all of them at that stage receiving stipends from UNTAET (or, in a minority of cases, from the NGOs) but not formally reemployed. The extent of the planned reduction in the number of facilities and staff is summarized in Table 2.

The first phase of the HSRDP also saw the implementation of the initial civil works program. It was decided to focus on community health centers to ensure one such facility in each of the territory's 65 subdistricts. It was planned that rehabilitation of health posts could be undertaken through community support at a later stage and that hospital reconstruction would also be delayed until a full assessment of need had been completed. A total of 23 sites were selected for construction and the design work tendered and completed. Construction of a new central pharmacy warehouse was also initiated, as was procurement of vehicles and equipment. The health policy development process was also started, but it stalled in mid-2001 for a variety of reasons.

With the formation in August 2000 of the First Transitional Government of East Timor, led by a cabinet that included East Timorese members, the IHA evolved into the DHS of the Government's Department of Social Affairs. The process of recruiting of East Timorese health civil servants was initiated in the last months of 2000 with the finalization of some 50 job descriptions for around 800 posts in 150 locations. This process, conducted

TABLE 2 Health Facilities and Staff (approximate numbers)

	Pre-1999	August 2000	Planned
Hospitals	12	6	5
Community health centers with beds	21	17	5
Community health centers without beds	46	52	64
Health posts	309	71	85
Total fixed facilities	406	146	158
Mobile clinics	60	Many*	116
Doctors/dentists	135	15	25
Specialists	20	0	1
Nurses/midwives/other	3,000+	1,800	1,430

*NGOs were conducting mobile clinics of different kinds ranging from one-off or infrequent visits to remote villages to regular scheduled clinics in fixed locations. The clinics also varied considerably in terms of the services provided. The definition and quantification of mobile clinics was therefore very difficult.

over the next six months, taxed to the limit the capacity of the DHS and the other relevant sections of UNTAET. A process had to be devised that was fair both to the older, long-serving nurses and auxiliaries and the younger, perhaps better qualified nurses and midwives. Long delays in the recruitment process, related in large part to the lack of sufficient professional expertise in the area of civil service development and recruitment in the transitional administration, added to the frustration of health workers, all of whom were anxious to know whether and where they would be employed. The delays affected the credibility of the DHS with some NGOs, which had to bear much of the discontent in the districts.

Phase II

In the middle of 2001 the HSRDP entered a second phase, which was the result of two concurrent exercises. The first was the preparation of the second budget of the transitional administration. In contrast to the exercise of the previous fiscal year, the 2001–2002 combined sources budget was, as the name suggests, an attempt to quantify and plan the use of funding from all sources. Preparation of this budget was a major and complex task. The combination of time constraints and the limited experience with such budgeting resulted in a limited role for the East Timorese members of the DHS in the process despite efforts to ensure full participation.

Nevertheless, the preparation of this budget was an important opportunity to reaffirm the principle of the sector-wide approach. The budget included remaining funds from the first TFET-funded project, an additional $12.6 million (US) planned for the second TFET-funded project, funds from the proposed transitional government's budget, and funds from bilateral donors and NGOs. Table 3 summarizes briefly and approximately the sources of funding and their agreed use during 2000–2001.

This combined sources budget and its associated work plans maintained the main elements of the HSRDP Phase I. It comprised three components for which 10 percent of funds could be reassigned without requiring new cabinet approval. The three components were: support to ongoing services, improvement in the scope and quality of services and support systems, and development of policy, regulations, and administrative systems.

During the period from April to September 2001, the DHS, using TFET funds, took over the financial support to NGOs in five districts. Although the funding levels were considerably reduced from those provided by other sources during the emergency phase, they were still very substantial. The DHS was providing an equivalent of $35,000 to $45,000 (US) per district per month for recurrent costs. An important question that faced the DHS was the manner in which technical support could be most efficiently provided to the district health services after September 2001, when the memorandum of understanding with the NGOs was to expire. For a number of reasons, including the cost and the inconsistent and variable quality of the support provided, it was considered undesirable simply to continue the existing system of support to one or two lead NGOs in each district.

At first, it was proposed that a competitive process be undertaken in which NGOs and other entities could bid to provide technical support to a group of two to four districts. After much discussion and a growing understanding, based on feedback from the field, of the support being provided at that time by the NGOs and its cost, the DHS decided against this option. By the third quarter of 2001, East Timorese district health management teams had been recruited in each of the districts, and it was not

TABLE 3 Main Sources and Uses of Funding

Source	Amount ($ millions US)	Main Activities/ Areas to Be Funded
ECHO	10–15 over 2 years	NGO support to basic services and district health plans (DHPs) up to mid-2001, some other projects
Consolidated Fund for East Timor	7.5 per year	Salaries, drugs/supplies, running costs
TFET I	12.7 over 2.5 years	Construction of community health centers (CHCs), vehicles, radio network, TA
TFET II	12.6 over 2.3 years	Hospital reconstruction, TA
UN agencies	?	IMCI, RH, immunization, communicable diseases, human resource development, other
Bilateral	At least 10 over 3 years	Mental, dental, HIV/AIDS, tuberculosis control, other

considered appropriate to put in place what would effectively have been another, nongovernmental layer in the system. The DHS extended funding to some NGOs that agreed to continue to provide services, at lower levels, to the end of 2001, but a phase-out strategy was announced and vigorously defended by the newly recruited leaders of the DHS, which in September 2001 became the Ministry of Health. It was decided that the ministry should use part of its TFET resources to hire directly the foreign expertise needed. Advertisements were placed in international media and a recruitment process initiated.

Achievements as of November 2001

Certainly the most important achievement by late 2001 was that in a little more than 18 months a fully East Timorese Ministry of Health had been put in place and over 800 health staff had been recruited and were working across the territory. This had been achieved with little unrest, despite the very significant downsizing of the health workforce and a certain tendency toward strikes and other employee protest in East Timor at the time. All community health centers were staffed and functioning, as were most of the health posts. However, the delays in civil service recruitment meant that staff at district level had been in place only for a short period by the time the phased withdrawal of NGO support was started. Rapid subsequent progress toward East Timorese district health teams' assuming district-level management can be considered another achievement. Only with time, however, will it be possible to judge whether the phasing out of international NGOs and their replacement with directly hired national expertise was well timed.

Since April 2000, most drugs had been provided to the health system by the central health authority (CHA),[2] from an agreed essential drug list, without major ruptures of stock. A new central pharmacy warehouse was entering the final stage of construction following international tendering of its design and construction. A consultant group had also been contracted to develop an autonomous medical supply system to ensure efficient procurement storage and distribution of pharmaceuticals and other medical supplies. A complete survey of health infrastructure and equipment had been completed, and 22 new health centers were under construction and major procurements of equipment completed or under way. Around 160 motorcycles and 35 four-wheel drive (4WD) vehicles had been procured for the health system, including appropriately equipped ambulances, and installation of a high-frequency radio network had been contracted after researching needs and experience elsewhere.

Policy and regulation development on pharmaceuticals and medical practice had been started through initial consultancy visits followed by a number of working sessions in which senior East Timorese health staff de-

---

[2]The term central health authority is introduced here for convenience to cover the IHA, the DHS, and the MOH which, in sequence, were the administration/government entities responsible for coordinating the health sector.

veloped proposals for submission to the Cabinet (later, the Council of Ministers). Nevertheless, considerable work remained to be done to reach agreement on the details of these complex policy areas.

In relation to disease-specific activities, one important achievement was the reestablishment of the National Tuberculosis Program implemented in collaboration with Caritas East Timor. Caritas Norway provided financial support and technical assistance, with additional technical input from WHO and the Northern Territory (of Australia) Health Services. Activities were coordinated under a memorandum of understanding with the Interim Health Authority elaborated in mid-2000. Over 6,000 cases of tuberculosis were detected and placed on treatment according to the directly observed treatment strategy. This went some way toward catching up on the treatment of the backlog of patients accumulated in recent years. By the end of 2001, the program covered all districts and many subdistricts. By that time, integrated management of childhood illness (IMCI) had been introduced through the adaptation of a Bahasa Indonesian version of the IMCI materials and the training of trainers. Similarly, decisions had been made about the initial approach to improving reproductive health services, with a focus on introducing and monitoring midwifery standards and identifying and addressing deficiencies.

With financial and technical support from AusAID, and within the framework of a sector-wide approach, projects were also under way on mental and dental health and HIV/AIDS prevention. Mental health activities initially focused on post-trauma recovery but were quickly expanded to start to address broader mental health needs, particularly in the capital. The initial project was followed up by a three-year project to develop services oriented to community prevention and basic services throughout the territory. The dental health project was developed using a similar two-stage process. Initial training of dental nurses aimed to provide basic palliative care in all districts. Two consultancy visits by joint UN teams in 2000 and 2001 assessed HIV/AIDS susceptibility and made initial plans for prevention activities. These were, however, slow to be implemented, and a short-term project was therefore initiated by the DHS with AusAID support. This focused on establishing an East Timorese working group to start to develop an approach to HIV/AIDS prevention in the particularly challenging religious and cultural context of East Timor, as well as on immediate prevention activities for vulnerable groups.

One notable overall achievement was the collaboration among all major actors in the health sector, including multilateral, bilateral, and UN technical agencies and NGOs to work within the framework of the sector-wide approach. There was little duplication of effort and relatively little competition for visibility. There was at times debate as to whether the HSRDP in East Timor constituted a true sector-wide approach. In the view of the authors, it fulfilled the most important aims of such an approach. Although all funding was not pooled into a common fund, there was sufficient pooling of funds to ensure a core program, and clear definition of the uses of other sources of funding ensured nonduplication of effort. This is reflected in Table 2, which shows the main sources of funding and the areas of work supported by each. The main objective of the sector-wide approach, to achieve one coherent program of development in the health sector, was very largely achieved.

Constraints and Failures

Despite what we believe to be the considerable achievements in the development of the health sector, there were also a number of areas in which progress was frustratingly slow or inadequate. It proved difficult, for example, to establish an effective health policy development process involving a range of health and nonhealth stakeholders. Among health staff with no previous experience in or responsibility for health policy, many of the issues that needed to be discussed may have seemed irrelevant and their presentation unnecessarily complex. The bigger policy issues were not of immediate obvious relevance to their own demands for employment, adequate salaries, and good working conditions, which were understandably their main preoccupations.

A small group inside and outside the CHA did show an interest in these topics and in trying to move the policy dialogue forward, but attempts at broader consultation were not successful. The process to develop policy adopted by the CHA with external technical assistance may not have been ideal in the context; although technically elegant and comprehensive and emphasizing national capacity for and ownership of the decision making, the process was viewed by most of the participants as too academic. Simple approaches to policy development when capacity is limited remain a challenge. They should keep in mind the broader context but focus, initially on issues of most concern to the stakeholders and those most likely to have long-lasting detrimental effects if not addressed early.

Another area in which progress was inadequate was the development of a comprehensive human resource development plan to guide priorities in medium- and long-term education and training. WHO provided strong technical support for meeting immediate needs, for example, in the preparation of more than 50 job descriptions and in defining a new cadre of nurse practitioners. Given the limited number of trained specialists and technicians, there was a pressing need to start training that could extend over several years. Dealing with the immediate needs for recruitment and capacity building left little time for developing the longer term plan. At the end of 2001, long-term planning for human resources remained an important need.

One area of delay that was particularly frustrating, because it should have been avoidable, was the civil works program, specifically the construction of community health centers. In this area the slower than planned progress was almost entirely due to inadequate capacity to handle procurement procedures and, in particular, the interaction between the World Bank procedures and those that were being developed and simultaneously applied by the UN transitional administration. Relative to the initial, admittedly extremely ambitious, civil works plan, initiation of construction was delayed by around one year. A central issue in the interagency differences in this area was the need to balance delegation of authority to the sectoral level (specifically to the senior staff that headed jointly the IHA and the program management unit of the TFET-funded project) with the need for centralized UN control and assumption of liability. Another aspect that complicated the process was the deriving of a tendering process, which gave emerging local companies the opportunity to compete while not excluding the potential economies of scale that might be offered by a large foreign contractor. Predictably this was a sensitive issue, with both foreign and local companies raising concerns. In one instance, there was a significant delay when a request for proposals was reissued because the first was deemed not to have resulted in effective competition.

As some of the rehabilitation carried out by NGOs restored health facilities to a level not compatible with the district health plans and because much of it was of a superficial nature, the IHA imposed limitations on rehabilitation activities. However, delays in the civil works program undermined the rationale for this approach. An early and detailed overview of the physical state of the infrastructure could have helped to guide rather than try to restrict NGO rehabilitation efforts.

As mentioned above, development of hospitals was intentionally postponed to the second phase of the HSRDP while concentrating on rehabilitating and reconstructing more peripheral services. In at least three districts, international NGOs had partially rehabilitated and were supporting hospitals that would be likely candidates to be downsized or closed in a rational health plan. This was one of the factors that obliged the CHA to make the unpopular decision to suspend further development of hospitals until a full assessment of needs and capacity and a comprehensive plan were developed. This was not achieved by the end of 2001, despite the political pressure created by this situation. Proposals developed by a consulting group were considered to be likely to lead to hospitals' consuming too large a proportion of the health budget, and a reassessment was called for.

A considerable achievement, obtained through the skillful negotiation of several senior East Timorese health staff, was the establishment of the National Centre for Health Education and Training. This brought together what had been in Indonesian times a number of independent educational and training centers for health professionals, for example, the nursing school, the nursing academy, and training institutions for sanitarians and nutritionists. An international NGO fully supported the rehabilitation of a previous complex of buildings to house the centre. However, these achievements were not followed with adequate technical and managerial support to the complex task of fusing the different activities into a well-functioning entity. This remains part of the human resource agenda that needed to be addressed.

Competing Objectives and Demands

One of the major challenges to the CHA in East Timor was the need to try to meet objectives and demands that were not all compatible. These demands were made by the public, by the political leadership, and by the donors. Table 4 summarizes some of the conflicting demands. Although these are not necessarily in direct contradiction, it should be apparent from the table that effort and resources would be applied with different priority depending on the relative importance given to each of these demands.

One area in which there was a marked contrast between the needs of the external assistance agencies and the needs and capacity of the CHA was in budgeting and planning. Not unreasonably, the donor agencies required a detailed 1-year budget and work plan, 1- to 2-year procurement plans, and a strategic plan covering a period from 4 to 10 years. The detailed combined-sources budget had to be broken down into "program" and "project" elements, by a series of standard expenditure codes and according

TABLE 4   Competing Goals for the Health Sector

Goals	Competing Goals
• Produce measurable results quickly	• Achieve transition to full East Timorese management
• Disburse funds quickly	• Ensure national decision making and full ownership
	• Focus on building capacity
	• Ensure sustainability
• Ensure a coherent sector-wide approach	• Accommodate individual donor needs
• Provide services to all now	• Improve scope and quality of services
• Develop health policies soon, before it is "too late"	• Consult widely on all policy issues
	• Stay flexible to avoid setting directions "too early"

to the source and security of funding. Even for experienced international staff, this was quite a demanding task.

The CHA, working with national staff with little or no previous experience or responsibility for budgeting and planning, had different priorities. It attempted to get each of the 14 units within the authority to set rather general 1–2 year objectives and then to make 3-month plans with a small number of well-defined achievable milestones that could be readily monitored. The planning of activities and achieving results were given far more importance than how to spend the money. The interest of the East Timorese unit heads in the financing was largely focused on the budgets for planned activities and on funds within their direct control. Few beyond the most senior staff were interested in the budgeting of funds over which they considered they had little influence.

Clearly, both the needs of the external assistance agencies and the internal needs of the CHA were legitimate. Almost inevitably, however, the former ended up being most time-consuming, particularly for the limited foreign expertise available.

Further demands were placed on the limited planning capacity of the CHA by the need to comment on and approve plans for collaboration from the three main UN agency partners prepared in different formats and covering different periods of time. These plans were designed to meet the agencies' institutional needs rather than accommodating to the program structure and priorities of the government.

STRENGTHS AND LIMITATIONS OF SOME OF THE MAIN ACTORS

The development of the health sector in East Timor involved multiple partners. We focus here on just three: UNTAET, the World Bank, and the NGOs. The roles of bilateral development assistance agencies and those of the UN system are not addressed here. Of the latter, the WHO, UNICEF, and UNFPA were the most involved and made many valuable contributions. The role played by WHO was evaluated by an independent team as part of a global study and is documented elsewhere (see Van der Heijden and Thomas, 2001).

One other group not examined in detail here meriting particular mention is the ETHPWG, formed within days of the conflict by the remaining senior East Timorese. The fact that this group was formed so early was critical. It was the national group most concerned about development of the health system, rather than the interests of one particular professional group. Its existence largely explains the ease with which the Interim Health Authority could be created by UNTAET and immediately achieve credibility, in contrast to the developments in some other sectors.

UN Transitional Administration in East Timor

It is impossible to fully summarize here the strengths and constraints of the UNTAET and its backup in New York from the DPKO. We have chosen several aspects that we believe to be important to the development of the sector. Arguably, the most important strength of the UNTAET was its legitimacy as the entity mandated to manage day-to-day matters and develop a government structure in East Timor. This conveyed full legitimacy, in turn, to the Interim Health Authority (and subsequently the DHS and later the first MOH), set up under UNTAET, to coordinate all matters related to health. Once it was recognized that the emergency phase was giving way to a development phase, this legitimacy was not challenged.

It is not obvious, however, that the role of UNTAET as the coordinator of development was best served by its institutional dependence on DPKO. The expertise of this entity did not appear to extend to a comprehensive understanding of the needs and priorities in the development of a health sector. This was reflected, for example, in the recruitment of staff for the health sector. Recent experience in any (post-) conflict situation, for example Kosovo, may have appeared to DPKO staff in New York to be a useful selection criterion, whereas extensive experience in health systems in developing countries similar to East Timor was what was really needed. A greater role for WHO in the recruitment of staff in similar situations may be desirable.

This was just one dimension of the incompatibility of the logic and needs of "development" and "peacekeeping." Another is what the authors came to see as the mission versus The Mission. We saw UNTAET's mission in the health sector as having two parts: restoring health services to the people of East Timor as rapidly as possible and developing and initiating a sustainable health system for the future. At times it seemed as if staff working in other parts of UNTAET saw their role as simply maintaining the machinery of the UN Mission, which was viewed by them as primarily one of peacekeeping, albeit a unique one with unusual elements. It was imperative in their view that this be done according to usual practice and UN rules for such situations, and there was minimal interest in the development tasks that UNTAET was mandated to carry out. This led to the sometimes absurd and often frustrating conflict between the aims and needs of the UN staff working with the East Timor transitional administration and those of staff working with the UNTAET Mission's administration. One example of the consequences was a distribution of transport and communication facilities that did not reflect the priority of the development activities. While the UNTAET administrative staff were all equipped with 4WD vehicles, often used only in the capital, the health sector staff, required to assess, organize, and supervise health activities throughout the country were not supplied with a vehicle for many months, despite frequent requests. A primary source of these disputes and inequities was different sources of funding, but they were also the result of different overall priorities.

In some cases, staff carrying out critical functions in other areas of the transitional administration appeared to have minimal experience in working in a development context and, in particular, had very limited understanding of the importance of the concept of sustainability.

Understandably, with a critical international community looking on, UNTAET was concerned both to produce results quickly and to maintain control, especially over the considerable resources being expended. The concern for control was heightened by the serious lack of individual accountability inherent in a situation in which staff turnover is extremely high. The lack of accountability of short-term staff for the medium- and long-term consequences of their action (or inaction) allowed inefficiency and incompetence in some essential support services to go unchecked. One direct reaction to this situation was a centralization of control such that even senior experienced UN staff working at the sectoral level had negligible control over resources. The health sector, for example, had no petty cash or imprest account of UN funds from which to make small purchases of goods and services. Centralized control, coupled with failure of certain central support services, was a constraint to achieving quick progress.

One function of the transitional administration that was, in our view, frequently very inefficient was procurement. Deficiencies were most apparent, and potentially most harmful, in the critical area of the procurement of pharmaceuticals, but they were also seen in areas as diverse as stationery and office equipment and recruitment of technical assistance. The authors believe that this is an area in which standards of performance must be defined and monitored.

The multinational nature of UNTAET was observed by us to be both a strength and a liability. On one hand, it guarded against the emerging government being exposed to only a single particular national perspective on any issue. On the other hand, certain complex activities were made more so when members of the teams implementing them came from very diverse experiential backgrounds.

The World Bank

It is difficult to exaggerate the importance of the role of the World Bank in the reconstruction of the health services in East Timor. It took a leading role in the early joint assessment of needs and in the development of the Health Sector Rehabilitation and Development Project (HRSDP), including the provision of high-quality technical assistance, managed the Trust Fund for East Timor (TFET) funds, and was responsive to and supportive of the CHA's needs throughout 2000-2001. The level of technical expertise provided by World Bank consultants was, with few exceptions, excellent, reflecting an unconstrained access to global expertise not seen in some other institutions limited by regional structures or strict fee payment policies. The World Bank was a strong advocate of the sector-wide approach and as controller of the pooled TFET funding was in a good position to encourage adherence to such an approach. Another strength of the World Bank is that its procedures for procurement and financial management, if sometimes bewilderingly complex, are at least well established. Perhaps most important, the World Bank had a competent task team in Washington committed to results and problem resolution and a supportive, politically astute, and accessible country office.

Working with the World Bank was nevertheless not without difficulties. As the custodian of the pooled TFET funds, the World Bank understandably felt pressure to show results to satisfy at least partially skeptical donors. This translated into what at times appeared to be a preoccupation with disbursement of funding potentially at the cost of other considerations. The pressure to spend could have led to hasty decisions on some important issues.

The most important area of constraint in working with the World Bank is summarized in one word: procurement. The first aspect of this was a concern with procurement rules that at times, and in some World Bank staff members, appeared obsessive. While a strong desire to guard against corruption and collusion is understandable, preoccupation with the avoidance of any suggestion of misprocurement can lead to an excessively rigid application of the rules.

Another dimension of the problem is that the procurement procedures have been developed for a context quite unlike the post-conflict rehabilitation and development situation, in which capacity in the interim government may be limited and urgency assumes a greater importance. The procedures may be well suited to the management of large loans over several years in an established system, but they are less well adapted to making available relatively small amounts of money needed quickly for action in a post-conflict context, in which managerial capacity of the client is, almost inevitably, limited.

The consequence of these first two procurement concerns, coupled with the very real need to get on with the job, was a series of time-consuming maneuvers designed to satisfy the requirements of the procurement rules while working within the capacity constraints. A more flexible interpretation of the rules—or better still, a set of adapted rules for post-conflict situations—would appear to be a more efficient way of arriving at the same result.

Given the need to work with existing World Bank procurement procedures and taking into account the wide range of goods and services that needed to be procured simultaneously, the specialist procurement capacity within the central health authority/program management unit (CHA/PMU) was grossly inadequate. This led to constant frustration that the considerable funds available could not be accessed and used as rapidly as had been planned. Even with procedures adapted for a similar situation, should these become available in the future, sufficient expert procurement capacity would be critical to quick progress.

NGOs

In the East Timor context, the NGOs operating in the health sector were almost entirely international, in most cases those that are well established internationally. Only two local NGOs, both with limited experience in health, played a role, although a number of church-affiliated clinics also provided services. This section focuses on the role of the international NGOs, but we cannot here fully describe the crucial role they played nor fully critique their performance.

An undoubted strength of the international NGOs is their ability to respond rapidly and their operational self-sufficiency. In East Timor, they moved in quickly, employed local health staff, and were the predominant source of health care, both at the primary and the hospital level for many months. Their contribution to saving lives and preventing suffering in East Timor was enormous. A second strength is the high level of commitment of most of their international staff and a willingness to work in remote areas and under tough conditions. A third very positive aspect of their presence in East Timor was their ultimately good cooperation with the CHA. This can probably be attributed to the very frequent contact between the NGOs and the CHA and the fact that they were recognized and treated as genuine partners in the development process. Without this close collaboration, the task of reestablishing a health system and transferring responsibility for it to East Timorese health professionals would have been very much more difficult.

Among the factors constraining the performance of the NGOs was a relative lack of development experience among their personnel. Many of the volunteers in East Timor were on their first mission, and very few personnel, including paid staff, had experience that would allow them to contribute fully to the development of the health system. Although some NGOs sought staff with public health qualifications and experience, this was the exception rather than the rule. In emergency situations, the provision of services under severe conditions often means high per capita expenditures and little concern for national ownership or sustainability. This perspective can be counterproductive in a context of development, in which the last two elements are of high priority.

A very high turnover of NGO staff, possibly important in emergency situations to avoid burnout, was a problem in East Timor, where close collaboration in medium-term activities was sought. It is encouraging that some NGOs recognized their limited capacity in development and voluntarily withdrew after the emergency phase and that others are specifically adapting themselves to post-conflict development. The authors believe, however, that the post-conflict aspect of the work should not be exaggerated. This can be a convenient label for NGOs (or indeed other institutions, including academic departments) looking for a new niche or to expand their role beyond emergencies (without necessarily changing their expertise). Many, perhaps most, of the problems facing the health sector in East Timor were those facing developing countries in general, including those that have not seen conflict in many years. Addressing these problems requires expertise in reform and management of health systems in developing countries; the post-conflict context is only one dimension of a complex problem.

Because some NGOs have conflict and emergency health experience in which conditions and logistics are usually difficult and security a major concern, one consequence is the relatively high cost of their operations. Under such circumstances, the norm for communication equipment and vehicles, for example, is higher than can be sustained in a longer term development effort. Similarly, in emergency situations, speed in procurement of drugs and supplies is of greater importance than such concerns as cost-effective purchasing (not to mention standardization and use of generic brands). In the East Timor context, the combined communication and logistics capacity of the NGOs working in the health sector dwarfed the capacity of the CHA. Funding for both NGOs and the CHA came ultimately from the same donors; cost-effectiveness and sustainability should have been one of their concerns.

A microcosm exemplifying the conflict between humanitarian assistance and the arguably equally humanitarian issue of sustainable development was the Dili General Hospital. The International Committee of the Red Cross moved in quickly and effectively to take on all aspects of the running of the territory's main referral hospital. It did so in a professional way and during 21 months provided resources that few, if any, institutions would have been able to match. Clearly it must be commended for providing such a valuable service to the people of East Timor. However, it did this at an estimated cost of $300,000 (US) per month, including in-kind contributions, an expenditure equivalent to almost half of the government's average monthly recurrent cost budget for health for 2001. Clearly, this was not a sustainable level of input. To its credit, the ICRC gave UNTAET 15 months advance warning of its eventual withdrawal, and its staff showed a good understanding of the need to scale back its operations progressively and to transfer responsibility to national staff as the date of departure approached.

Another difficult aspect of the NGO involvement in East Timor resulted from the enormous variability in capacity of the NGOs and the need of some to compete vigorously for funding. The need to compete and to be seen to be performing led to considerable overstatement of capacity in some cases. While some NGOs do have true professional experience in and resources for the rehabilitation of health facilities, for example, others claimed to have such expertise but, in fact, made shoddy repairs that did not last long after the photographs had been taken for the head office and the donors. It was difficult for the CHA to assess, a priori, the expertise of different NGOs, including some with excellent self-promotional skills.

From the perspective of the CHA, the best NGOs were those with a clear institutional definition of their intended role in East Timor, that worked in collaboration with the CHA, that knew their true capacity and limitations, that ensured they had capable staff on the ground, and that had sufficient financial resources to achieve their objectives. In contrast, the most problematic NGOs were those that had a limited, often general management presence in the territory and were seeking a role and official endorsement for it that they would then use to seek funds. While claiming to be more responsive to the needs of the CHA, such NGOs usually wasted its time and achieved little.

TOO MUCH MONEY TOO SOON?

One of the inevitable conclusions of the experience in East Timor in 2000–2001 can be summarized, if oversimply, as "money drives everything." It is clear that without money in sufficient quantity, nothing could be achieved and that it is important to exploit politically driven interest in funding a particular effort while it lasts. It is also true that the awareness that funding will start to decline and the related need to spend available money quickly can have distorting effects.

One of the reasons that relatively large amounts of money were available early in East Timor was the consolidated appeal for funding in the emergency phase. Given the relative political attractiveness of emergencies and the undeniable health needs in such situations, a significant amount of money was quickly available to the health sector. The fact that, even by mid- to late 2000, much of the money had not been spent suggests that the emergency funds surpassed the absorptive capacity. This led to some of the funded entities, not wanting to be left with unspent funds, finding creative ways of using them within the stipulated guidelines but with little relevance to the true needs.

A particular consequence of the availability of emergency funding to the health sector was the rehabilitation of some health facilities, including hospitals, by NGOs before any plan for health facility location and size had been completed. Rehabilitation is popular with donors to emergency situations (in part because it is visible and can absorb considerable resources) and certainly some rehabilitation is essential, but early unplanned or poorly executed rehabilitation can produce difficulties for the future government.

Another cause for the relative overabundance of early funding is that "size matters." There are few incentives at any level for a manager of funds to opt for a smaller budget and activity portfolio. Prestige (and to some extent promotion) in international agencies and the development banks is undoubtedly linked, in part, to the size of the budgets handled by an individual. An NGO head of mission is likely to be viewed well by the head office if he or she is able to secure generous funding from donors on the ground even if it exceeds the real needs or the organization's capacity to spend effectively. There are few incentives for requesting or spending less money than is available. Another cause of the pressure to spend money early is the "use it or lose it" financing approach taken by most funding and financial management entities.

One particularly problematic effect of the oversupply of funds is the distortion of local salary scales. In East Timor, international NGOs in the health sector by and large acted responsibly in this regard, adopting a shared voluntary salary scale. Nevertheless, payment of high salaries to local staff by some agencies, including those of the UN, was one of the main factors contributing to discontent with "government" salaries.

A particular reason for the availability of very considerable resources in the East Timor context was the needs of the UN peacekeeping operation. One example that affected the health sector was the needs of the UN peacekeepers for continuously available medical air evacuation services. Given that the entity providing these was paid for a minimum number of flying hours and that military demand proved to be relatively low, these services were available to the civilian population. While meeting an obvious humanitarian need, this introduced a distortion to the health system and may have created expectations that clearly cannot be met in the future.

The sudden availability in East Timor of large amounts of external funding created an artificial situation in which unrealistic expectations could arise and unsustainable services be put in place. This will make the task of the future leadership more difficult when financial and other resources decline to more realistic levels. More generally, the availability of high levels of resources may have led to the exposure of East Timorese counterparts to bad examples in terms of choices in the use of funds and in use of official resources, for example, transport. This occurred at a time whenthe international community, perhaps above all, should have been providing a model to the future leaders of the new East Timor.

WHAT COULD BE DIFFERENT NEXT TIME?

The complexity of post-conflict situations and the differences from one setting to another make it difficult to come up with succinct and generalizable recommendations. Based on our experience in East Timor in 2000–2001, we make the following suggestions. We hope that readers' analysis of the preceding text may also provide lessons that are not specifically mentioned here.

Specific suggestions directed at UN transitional administrations, the World Bank, international NGOs, and those who provide funding are made below. We start here with some more general suggestions.

The authors feel strongly that a sector-wide approach to planning and coordinating the rehabilitation and development of the health sector is essential from the outset. Whatever management challenges it may produce and whatever criticisms it may draw from donors and others with particular interests, it is the best option for ensuring the coherent development of the health sector. The alternative of a series of semi-independent projects, each with its own management and coordination burden, is likely to prove very difficult for the future Ministry of Health to control and integrate at a later time.

National control of the rehabilitation and development process should not be compromised for the sake of more rapid decision making and progress. All actors in the health sector should accept from the outset the legitimacy of the interim government, especially its national members.

Similarly, no compromise should be made concerning a deliberate focus on sustainability. Ignoring sustainability in order to make quick gains is likely to produce long-standing difficulties for the future government. Every effort should be made to move quickly from a humanitarian assistance approach to one of sustainable development. Prolongation of the emergency phase should be avoided. In this regard, it is important to ensure that arguments for high, short-term inputs based on humanitarian concerns do not automatically override long-term considerations. The fact that humanitarian relief assistance is currently much easier to obtain than development assistance is a concern, as the source of the funding can determine the nature of the inputs.

As early as possible, a full and professional assessment of the physical health infrastructure should be conduct by an expert team. This is likely to prove more important than a rapid assessment of the health situation, especially in situations in which the latter is to a large extent predictable. Based on this assessment, a crude and conservative plan for future health facilities should be made and communicated to all concerned. This will inevitably be revised, as long-term funding realities become apparent and health policy is developed. It should be made clear that decisions concerning rehabilitation, construction, placement, size, and services available at health facilities are to be made by the interim government.

Without jeopardizing the above areas, the authors feel that compromises should be made in procedures, in the time frame for producing results, in centralized control, and in application of unrealistically high standards of quality. In all of these areas it is important to recognize the constraints of the post-conflict situation and the inevitably limited capacity of the emerging government. Procedures—for example, those for procurement, budgeting, and financial management—should be adapted to this context while still ensuring an acceptable level of accountability.

Significant benefit might be gained in the long term by removing some of the pressure to produce results quickly. More emphasis should be placed on the durability and sustainability of achievements than on rapid disbursement of funds and quick results. Nevertheless, more could be achieved early with some loosening of central control, particularly in the UN system. Sectoral experts from the system who have a track record of responsible management should be given greater managerial independence, including over financial resources. This should include the freedom to organize and fund training activities, recruit short-term staff, and make purchases of minor supplies, without passing through the central procurement process.

While concern with the quality of service provision is important, setting unrealistic targets in this regard too soon can be a barrier to providing basic services to all quickly. Effort to put national systems in place to achieve long-term improvements in the quality of health care should not be given priority until basic services are widely available. This also provides time for standardizing guidelines and developing human resource development plans.

One serious constraint to the health sector in East Timor was the very delayed recruitment of national health staff. In situations in which a health service has to be recreated, senior health staff should be recruited as soon as possible so that, from a secure position, they can participate fully in the development process, including the recruitment of staff at lower levels. It is critical that this happens simultaneously in all sectors, so that national staff can interact with their national counterparts in other sectors rather than foreign substitutes. This in turn should lead to better cross-sectoral collaboration, which was a weakness in East Timor. The transition period is a critical opportunity for rapid capacity development that can only be achieved if national staff are allowed to assume genuine responsibility and are provided support to meet it.

From their interaction with other parts of the UNTAET, the authors have the following recommendations for future administrations. First is the importance of securing key central administrative functions in the interim government with teams that are truly expert in the field concerned. In such areas as legal systems, civil service recruitment, and government procurement, it may be useful to have expertise supplied by an entity from a particular UN member state rather than through multinational teams. The budget office of the transitional administration in East Timor was one very successful example of this approach. Trying to put together a key service with people from many different national systems may be extremely inefficient, as was demonstrated in certain areas in East Timor. Structuring a civil service and recruiting staff for it, for example, require real expertise. Delays in this can have a huge impact on staff morale and the progress of system development. Compromise on the UN principle of a multinational staff could greatly facilitate some largely administrative functions for which diversity of input may be of little benefit.

Efficiency could be improved and a lot of frustration avoided by the establishment of a dedicated UN problem-solving and lesson accumulation team on the ground working across sectors. This would lead to addressing of systemic issues rather than ad hoc resolution of problems in one sector only to have them arise again in another. Much of the inefficiency in East Timor could be traced to minor issues, but no entity was charged with the responsibility and authority to identify and definitively resolve such issues.

Regarding the World Bank, the authors would like to propose adaptation of procedures, particularly for procurement, to the post-conflict setting. The adapted procedures need not apply to all funds but should allow less-constrained spending on some elements of the rehabilitation and development program. Either agreement should be reached on acceptable adaptations to allow easier spending of some portion of the World Bank controlled funds, or a greater role for bilateral funding should be accepted and clearly defined, especially for areas in which more straightforward and rapid fund dispersement may be needed.

Whether or not such changes are made, the World Bank should ensure more support to program implementation. In particular, it is critical to ensure that the PMU has adequate procurement capacity, especially early, especially for civil works.

Transparent and frequent explanations of where the money is going is critical for maintaining good collaboration with and a good image of the World Bank. This could be coupled with less focus on disbursement and more focus on what is being achieved. In order for the World Bank to adopt such an approach, its donors should, in turn, do so.

It is difficult to make a succinct set of recommendations concerning NGOs, in part because of the diversity of their nature and competence. Among the international NGOs that can be considered the leaders in the field, there does seem to be an active process of self-analysis and attempts at reform. We encourage this. NGOs should be clear about their particular strengths and stick to situations in which they are appropriate. NGOs with expertise in emergency situations may not contribute effectively to health system development. In any event, it would be useful for staff of NGOs working in post-conflict situations to be briefed on the essential aspects of sustainable development.

With respect to the possible initial oversupply of resources, it may be important to examine the emergency appeal process. While it may be important to capitalize on initial interest, it is equally important that the funds raised be used to maximum effect. From the outset it is important to consider what will happen after the post-conflict crisis is over and a country is left to its own devices and perhaps struggling with its new independence.

The donor community may be generous in the first few years following the conflict, but experience shows that it takes much longer to rebuild a country or even to implement an initial development program. Absorptive capacity may be low initially and take several years to grow. Proportionately more of the resources may be needed in the years following the immediate post-conflict response. A longer time horizon for countries emerging from conflict may be needed. This should not perpetuate the emergency phase or delay the imperatives of ownership and capacity building. It could be facilitated by allowing funds raised in the first flush of donor support to be put in reserve, for example in sector-specific trust funds, for use when capacity and development needs are increasing.

Finally, it is important to put in place mechanisms for documenting and learning from experience in post-conflict situations. Those directly involved in the support of rebuilding efforts are usually too busy to spend time documenting the process and may not be objective. Nevertheless, their experience in confronting practical issues under difficult circumstances could be extremely valuable and should be captured. Although there will be many situation-specific factors, it is likely that there will be many more common issues. Unless experience is recorded and analyzed, changing the way various organizations do business, people will keep repeating the same mistakes and running into the same obstacles. We hope that some of the experiences of East Timor and the above suggestions that are drawn from them will be of use in reforming approaches to countries in post-conflict situations.

REFERENCES

United Nations Country Team
    2000   *Common Country Assessment for East Timor: Building Blocks for a Nation.* East Timor: United Nations.
Van der Heijden, T., and K. Thomas
    2001   Review of WHO's Emergency Response in East Timor. (unpublished manuscript), Geneva, World Health Organization.

Appendix
A
Chronology of Selected Developments and Events in East Timor

POLITICAL DEVELOPMENTS AND THE
ESTABLISHMENT OF GOVERNMENT

April 25, 1974: Revolution of the Red Carnations in Portugal allows the process of decolonization and the establishment of political parties in East Timor.

August 12, 1975: Coup d'état by the Christian Democratic Union of Timor (UDC) starts a fratricidal war between UDC followers and Revolutionary Front of Independent East Timor (FRETILIN) supporters.

November 28, 1975: Proclamation of the independence of the Democratic Republic of Timor Leste by FRETILIN.

December 7, 1975: Indonesian army forces invade East Timor.

July 17, 1976: Indonesian President Soharto signs the bill of integration incorporating East Timor as Indonesia's 27th province.

1975–1999: Struggle for independence initially under the leadership of FRETILIN and from 1987 under the National Council of the Maubere Resistance (CNRM) followed by the National Council of Timorese Resistance (CNRT) from 1998. The armed struggle is carried out by National

Liberation Army of East Timor (FALINTIL) complemented by the clandestine resistance and continuous efforts on the diplomatic front internationally.

August 30, 1999: Popular Consultation under the auspices of the United Nations Mission in East Timor (UNAMET) on the future status of the territory. With a 98 percent rate of participation, the majority of voters (78.5 percent) rejects autonomy (within Indonesia) thus opting for independence.

September 4, 1999: Official announcement of the election results. Pro-Indonesian militia groups backed by the Indonesian Army, who have practiced intimidation in the run-up to the election, launch a systematic campaign of violence and destruction. Forced deportation and displacement resulted in some 200,000 refugees in West Timor and other parts of Indonesia.

September 15, 1999: The Security Council Resolution 1264 establishes the International Force in East Timor (INTERFET) to restore peace and security in the territory and to assist UN operations and humanitarian programs.

October 25, 1999: Security Council Resolution 1272 establishes the UN Transitional Administration of East Timor (UNTAET) with the mandate to keep peace and to "exercise all legislative and executive authority" in the administration of East Timor.

July 15, 2000: Establishment of the First Transitional Government of East Timor sharing power among eight cabinet members: four East Timorese and four UNTAET international staff.

September 20, 2000: INTERFET forces arrive in East Timor and within days restore security.

August 30, 2001: General elections to elect 88 members for a Constituent Assembly responsible for drafting, debating, and adopting the first constitution of East Timor.

September 15, 2001: Inauguration of the Constituent Assembly of East Timor.

September 20, 2001: Establishment of the Second Transitional Government of East Timor and its Council of Ministers.

March 22, 2002: Approval of the Constitution of the Democratic Republic of East Timor by the Constituent Assembly representatives in plenary session.

May 20, 2002: East Timor proclaims its independence.

SELECTED DEVELOPMENTS IN THE HEALTH SECTOR, 2000–2001

February 16, 2000: Establishment of the Interim Health Authority (IHA) by UNTAET.

April 2000: First Joint Donor Mission led by the World Bank and IHA.

August 2000: The IHA evolves into the Division of Health Services (DHS) following the formation of the First Transitional Government of East Timor and the associated East Timor Transitional Administration (ETTA).

November 2000: Second Joint Donor Mission for the health sector.

May 2001: Third Joint Donor Mission for the health sector.

September 20, 2001: Dr. Rui Maria de Araujo is appointed as the first minister of health of East Timor following the establishment of the Second Transitional Government.

Appendix B

Illustrative Memorandum of Understanding for Implementation of a District Health Plan

This is an example of a memorandum of understanding between the Division of Health Services (DHS) of the East Timor Transitional Administration and any particular NGO. XXX indicates the occurrences of customized information.

A   Introduction

1. This letter of agreement between NGO-HSP and the Division of Health Services (DHS) of the East Timor Transitional Administration details a mutually agreed upon cooperative framework for the provision of basic health services in XXX District, East Timor, for the period _____ 2000 to _____ 2001.

2. The agreement reached is based on a consultative process involving NGO-HSP, DHS (at the central and regional level), other national and international NGOs, East Timorese health personnel, and XXX District community representatives. The consultative process has produced the XXX District Health Plan (dated _____ 2000), which was reviewed and agreed upon in principle by DHS.

   (1) To avoid the duplication of services and the installation of services that may be unsustainable in the future and to respect minimum standards

for health service delivery in East Timor for the transition period, guidelines for District Health Plans were agreed upon in May/June 2000 and supplemented by additional guidelines in July 2000, which are attached as Appendix I.

(2) The District Health Plan for XXX District, prepared by NGO-HSP and reviewed and agreed upon by DHS, details the range of services agreed upon by both signatories to this Letter of Agreement to be provided in compliance with the attached guidelines.

B   Agreement

1.   NGO-HSP agrees to implement the agreed plan with due diligence, to keep DHS informed of implementation progress through quarterly progress reports, and to seek DHS prior agreement to any substantial departure from the plan in schedule, content, and/or budget. The agreed upon distribution of fixed facilities, the overall number of staff to be paid by DHS, and an initial distribution of staff are provided in Appendix II.

2.   NGO-HSP agrees that it will seek prior written approval from DHS concerning all matters related to :

- distribution and location of all fixed and mobile facilities,
- any construction, reconstruction and/or rehabilitation of health facilities,
- numbers and distribution of staff, including voluntary staff and those paid by sources other than DHS, and
- agreements with third parties.

3.   Where not explicitly detailed in the XXX District Health Plan, NGO-HSP undertakes by signing this Letter of Agreement that, in addition to the activities detailed in the District Health Plan, it will:

- participate, under the guidance of DHS, in the acceleration of priority activities, such as immunization, vitamin A supplementation, TB control, and health promotion,
- inform the DHS in advance of any pharmaceutical supplies or equipment obtained from sources other than the Central Pharmacy Warehouse/Autonomous Medical Store, whether purchased or donated,

• follow any DHS needs assessment, guidelines, and training plans for on-the-job and short-term training to develop the capacity of East Timorese health personnel,

• maintain records of patient contacts and other services using national protocols as they become available, and use a standard reporting format prescribed by DHS,

• maintain financial accounts in accordance with internationally recognized practices,

• provide a six-monthly consolidated report of expenditures by categories to be specified by DHS, and

• not enter into any third party agreement where the DHS may, as a result of that agreement, be liable for any claims, debt, damage or demand arising out of the implementation of the district health plan.

4.   In recognition of the above, DHS agrees: (1) to provide salary and benefits at the official ETTA levels for personnel as detailed in Appendix II, (2) to provide pharmaceuticals and supplies in accordance with nationally determined levels ensuring an equitable distribution (from all sources) across all districts, and (3) further undertakes to finalize by November 2000, in close consultation with NGO-HSP and within the framework of the agreed XXX District Health Plan, the level of support to be provided by DHS for transport, communications, and related operational costs.

C   Monitoring and Evaluation

1.   Implementation of the District Health Plan for XXX District will be monitored by DHS using quantitative and qualitative indicators.

2.   NGO-HSP will provide DHS with a quarterly report of implementation progress in the format provided in Appendix III of this agreement.

3.   Should the number of beneficiaries of the District Health Plan significantly change from the number originally envisaged, or if for any reason, changed circumstances reduce or increase the need for financial and/or other inputs, DHS shall be immediately informed so that, after mutual consultation, DHS may adapt its participation to the new situation.

D   Termination of the Agreement

1. This agreement will terminate on _____ 2001, at which time a further agreement for the period _____ 2001 to _____ 2002 based on a revised, or new District Health Plan for the XXX District may be prepared by mutual agreement between the undersigned in consultation with appropriate representation of East Timorese health personnel and community representatives of the XXX District.

2. The agreement may be terminated at an earlier date should NGO-HSP fail to address, within thirty (30) days of receiving written advice from the DHS, any substantial departure from the framework agreement in the XXX District Health Plan.

Agreed, this day _____ 2000

_____	_____
Authorized Representative	Authorized Representative
of NGO-HSP	of DHS

Attachments :
     Appendix I   Guidelines for the District Health Plan
     Appendix II   Personnel and Facilities to be provided by DHS
     Appendix III Quarterly Reporting Format

FURTHER GUIDELINES FOR REVISION OF DHP, JULY 2000

1. It should be recalled that the *access target* by September 2001 is 90 percent. Access to a mobile clinic within 2 hours walk *twice per week* will be considered as access to a "permanent" source of services.

2. There will be *one fixed facility* (generally a CHC—without beds) *in each subdistrict*. This may be functioning only as a HP at present but can serve as the center for subdistrict activities including mobile clinics.

3. In general, during the transition period (i.e., the period of the current DHPs), to maintain flexibility in placement of permanent structures, the IHA prefers *the use of more mobile clinics and fewer HPs.*

4. The IHA prefers *the use of motorcycles (or horses) rather than 4WD vehicles for mobile clinics*. If 4WD vehicles are used, there must be a clear justification.

5. In general, mobile clinics should be operated from the subdistrict CHC. For the sake of clarity, mobile clinics operating from HPs will be referred to as *"outreach services."*

6. *Current HPs* should continue to function where they do not exceed the basic access criteria. Those that exceed the access criteria should be closed.

7. *New or reopened HPs* should only be established in villages or groups of villages that a mobile clinic can not reach within 1 hour, that have a collective population of 1,000 or more, and that are justified by the workload.

8. *No more (new or expanded) inpatient facilities (beds) should be established anywhere without prior written approval from the IHA.* This will, in general, not be given within the context of the current DHP negotiations. In any case, no new inpatient facilities will be paid for by NGO funding sources. Where needed they will be supported by the IHA.

9. *Planned staffing levels* for staff to be paid for by the IHA should be within the ceiling provided for the district. In addition, HSPs may, with other sources of funding, employ an additional number of health professional staff equivalent to no more than 10 percent of the ceiling and an equivalent number of administrative staff

10. For a CHC, a maximum staff of five should be considered. As a guide, this would be one nurse manager, two nurse/midwives, two nurses but there should be some flexibility.

11. IHA-supported staff for inpatient facilities will be at the number foreseen for the facility in the future, not at the current unapproved level of functioning. Additional staff must be paid by the HSP.

12. HPs should be staffed by one nurse/midwife. Any additional staff would require clear justification.

13. Each expatriate staff should have an assigned East Timorese counter-part.

14. Expatriate staffing should be according to the following guidelines:

Districts without a hospital	- one coordinator (doctor or MPH)
	- one doctor (if no East Timorese doctor available)
	- one nurse/midwife as trainer
Hospitals	- one manager
	- one doctor (if no East Timorese doctor available)
	- one nurse/midwife as trainer
Administrative staff	- up to two persons (including those in Dili)

Appendix
C

Bibliographic Materials

SELECTED BIBLIOGRAPHY FOR EAST TIMOR

Asian Development Bank
  2000 Strategic Planning Framework and Budget Rehabilitation, Development and
        Management of the Water and Sanitation Sector 2000–2003. Manila,
        Phillippines: Asian Development Bank.
Dunn, J.
  1996 *Timor: A People Betrayed.* Sidney: ABC Books.
Joint Assessment Mission
  1999 Building a Nation: A Framework for Reconstruction and Development. Joint
        Assessment Mission of specialists from East Timor, bilateral donors countries,
        UN agencies, Asian Development Bank, World Bank, November. Background
        paper coordinated by World Bank, Washington, DC.
Ospina, S., and T. Hohe
  2002 *Traditional Power Structures and Local Governance in East Timor: A Case Study of
        the Community Empowerment Project.* Geneva: Graduate Institute of Development
        Studies.
Pedersen, J., and M. Arneberg, eds.
  1999 *Social and Economic Conditions in East Timor.* New York and Oslo: Columbia
        University, and Fafo Institute of Applied Social Science.
United Nations Country Team
  2000 *Common Country Assessment for East Timor: Building Blocks for a Nation.*
        November. Available online at: <http://www.undp.east-timor.org/publications/
        Cca.pdf>

United Nations Transitional Administration in East Timor

2000 Timor Consolidated Appeal Process (CAP). Humanitarian Assistance and Emergency Rehabilitation Pillar (HEAR). Dili, East Timor: United Nations Transitional Administration in East Timor.

World Bank

2000 Project Appraisal Document for Health Sector Rehabilitation and Development. Phase I. Dili, East Timor.

2001 Project Appraisal Document for Health Sector Rehabilitation and Development. Phase II. Dili, East Timor.

World Health Organization

2001a *Collaboration in East Timor.* Dili, July 2000.

2001b Timor Health Sector Situation Report, March 2000.

2001c WHO's Contribution to Health Sector Development in East Timor, January 2000–May 2001. Background Paper for Donors' Meeting on East Timor. Canberra, 14-15 June 2001. Dili.

OTHER RESOURCES ON
POST-CONFLICT RECONSTRUCTION

Addison, T.

1998 *Rebuilding Post-Conflict Africa: Reconstruction and Reform.* The United Nations University. World Institute for Development Economics Research.

Anderson, M.B.

1996 *Do No Harm: Supporting Local Capacities for Peace Through Aid,* Collaborative for Development Action, Cambridge, MA, April.

Anderson, M., and P. Woodrow

1989 *Rising from the Ashes: Development Strategies in Times of Disaster.* Boulder, CO: Westview Press.

Astolfi, A.

1999 *Reconstruction apres la guerre: L'exemple de Pakrac, Croatie.* Paris: Harmattan; Geneve: Institut d'etudes sociales (IES).

Aysan, Y., and I. Davis

1993 *Rehabilitation and Reconstruction.* Module prepared for the Disaster Management Training Programme, UNDP/DHA.

Azam, J.-P., D. Bevan, P. Collier, S. Dercon, J.W. Gunning, and S. Pradhanet

1994 *Some Economic Consequences of the Transition from Civil War to Peace,* Policy Research Working Paper 1392. Washington, DC: World Bank.

Ball, N., and K.F. Campbell

1998 *Complex Crisis and Complex Peace: Humanitarian Coordination in Angola.* New York: United Nations, Office for the Coordination of Humanitarian Affairs.

Ball, N., and T. Halevy

1996 *Making Peace Work: The Role Of The International Development Community.* Washington, DC: Overseas Development Council.

Balladelli, P.
    2000   *Communicating Best Practice in Humanitarian Health: The Experience of WHO in Postconflict.* Geneva: WHO/EHP/EHA.
Barakat, S., M. Ehsan, and A. Strand
    1994   *NGOs and Peace-Building in Afghanistan.* Post-War Reconstruction and Development Unit (PRDU), University of York.
Barnabas G., and A. Zwi
    1997   Health policy development in wartime: Establishing the baito health system in Trigray, Ethiopia. *Health Policy and Planning* 12(1): 38–49.
Bevan, D., and S. Pradhan
    1994   Fiscal Aspects of the Transition from War to Peace: with Illustrations from Uganda and Ethiopia. In Azam et al. (eds.), *Some Economic Consequences of the Transition from Civil War to Peace.* Policy Research Working Paper 1392. Washington, DC: World Bank.
Birkeland, N.
    2000   *War, Environment and Forced Migration in Angola. Recovery and Development after Conflict and Disaster.* Trondheim, Norway: Norwegian University of Science and Technology.
Boyce, J.K.
    1995   Adjustment toward peace: An introduction. *World Development* 23(12): 2067–2077.
    1995   External assistance and the peace process in El Salvador. *World Development* 23(12): 2101–2116.
Boyce, J., ed.
    1996   *Economic Policy for Building Peace.* Boulder, CO: Lynne Rienner.
Bower, H.
    2002   *Reconstructing Afghanistan's Health System: Are Lessons Being Learned From The Past?* London: London School of of Health and Tropical Medicine, Masters of Science Project.
Bradbury, M.
    1998   Normalizing the crisis in Africa. *Journal of Humanitarian Assistance,* Cambridge: University of Cambridge.
Brück, T., E. FitzGerald, and A. Grigsby
    2000   *Enhancing the Private Sector Contribution to Post-War Recovery in Poor Countries. QEH Working Paper Series.* Oxford: Queen Elizabeth House.
Burnham, P.
    1990   *The Political Economy of Postwar Reconstruction.* New York: St. Martin's Press.
Bush, K.
    1995   Towards a balanced approach to rebuilding war-torn societies. *Canadian Foreign Policy* 3 (Winter).
Canadian International Development Agency (CIDA)
    1998   *Conflict Prevention and Post Conflict Reconstruction: A Matrix of Analytical Tools Available Internationally for Peacebuilding and Donor Coordination.* Ottawa: CIDA Peacebuilding Unit.

Canadian Public Health Association and the London School of Hygiene and Tropical Medicine

    2000 Symposium on post-conflict health and health systems: Issues and challenges. March 19-21, Ottawa, Canada.

Carbonnier, G.

    1998 *Conflict, Postwar Rebuilding and the Economy: A Critical Review of the Literature.* Occasional Paper No. 2. Geneva: UNRISD and War-Torn Societies Project.

    1999 The challenges of rebuilding war-torn economies. In K.R. Spillman and J. Krause (eds.) *International Security Challenges in a Changing World.* New York: Peter Lang.

Chanda, N.

    1986 *Brother Enemy—The War after the War.* New York: Macmillan.

Charters, D., ed.

    1994 *Peacekeeping and the Challenge of Civil Conflict Resolution.* Fredericton, Canada: Centre for Conflict Studies, University of New Brunswick.

Cliff, J.

    1993 Donor dependence or donor control? The case of Mozambique. *Community Development Journal* 28: 237–244.

Collier, P.

    1999 *The Challenge of Ugandan Reconstruction.* Washington, DC: World Bank.

    2000 Policy for Post-conflict Societies: Reducing the Risks of Renewed Conflict. Paper prepared for the Economics of Political Violence Conference, March 18–19. Washington, DC

    2002 *Aid, Policy and Growth in Post-Conflict Countries.* Development Research Group (DECRG), World Bank, CPR Dissemination Notes No. 2, April 2002. Available online at <http://wbln0018.worldbank.org/Networks/ESSD/icdb.nsf/D4856 F112E805DF4852566C9007C27A6/05A192FD7A1FAFC985256BCA0057 BC41/$FILE/CPR+2+Legal.pdf>.

Collier, P., and A. Hoeffler

    2002 *Aid, Policy, and Growth in Post-Conflict Societies.* Washington, DC: World Bank.

Cox, M.

    1998 *Strategic Approaches to International Intervention in Bosnia and Herzegovina.* Geneva: Centre for Applied Studies in International Negotiation.

    2000 *State Building and Post-Conflict Reconstruction: The Lessons from Bosnia.* Geneva: CASIN. Available online at <http://www.casin.ch/pdf/cox.pdf>.

Cox, M., and C. Harland

    2000 Displaced persons and institutional mechanisms in post-conflict societies: the case of Bosnia and Herzegovina. In *Consultation on the International Complaints Mechanisms Available to Refugees and Internally Displaced Persons.* Oxford: Oxford University.

Crocker, C.A., F.O. Hampson, and P. Aall, eds.

    1996 *Managing Global Chaos: Sources of and Responses to International Conflict.* Washington DC: United States Institute of Peace Press.

Cullen, M., and J. Mendelson Forman

    1998 *Conflict Prevention and Post-Conflict Reconstruction: Perspectives and Prospects.* Available online at: <http://www-unix.oit.umass.edu/~educ870/PostConflict/ resources/Colleta-PostConflict-Rcnstrctn-98.pdf>.

Davies, L.
2000   Balkans briefing 6. Picking up the pieces: Reflections on the initial stages of the reconstruction of the health care system in Kosovo, July 1999. *Journal of Epidemiology and Community Health* 54: 705–707.

Doornbos, M., and A. Tesfal, eds.
1999   *Post-Conflict Eritrea: Prospects for Reconstruction and Development.* Asmara, Eritrea: The Red Sea Press.

Duffield, M.
1994   Complex emergencies and the crisis of developmentalism. *IDS Bulletin* 25(3): 37–45.

Dunn, J.
1996   *Timor: A People Betrayed.* Sydney: ABC Books.

EIU
1993   *Angola to 2000. Prospects for Recovery.* London: The Economist Publications Limited.

Forsythe, V.
1994   Health care in situations of post-conflict transition: A preliminary review of the Palestinian situation. London School of Hygiene and Tropical Medicine. Unpublished document.

Frieden, J.
1991   External support and management of the health sector in Mozambique. Unpublished draft report. Cambridge: Harvard University.

Garfield, R.M.
1989   War-related changes in health and health services in Nicaragua. *Social Science and Medicine* 28(7): 669–676.

Goodhand, J., and P. Atkinson
2001   *Conflict and Aid: Enhancing the Peace-building Impact of International Engagement—A synthesis of findings from Afghanistan, Liberia and Sri Lanka. International Alert.* Available online at: <www.international-alert.org>.

Goodhand, J., and D. Hulme
1997   *NGOs And Peace Building In Complex Political Emergencies: An Introduction.* Manchester: University of Manchester.
1999   From wars to complex political emergencies: understanding conflict and peace-building in the new world disorder. *Third World Quarterly* 20(1): 13–26.

Goyens, P., D. Porignon, E. Mugisho Soron' Gane, R. Tonglet, P.H. Hennart, and H.L. Screw
1996   Humanitarian aid and health services in Eastern Kivu, Zaire: Collaboration or Competition? *Journal of Refugee Studies* 9(3): 268–280.

Haughton, J.
1997a   The Reconstruction of a War-Torn Economy: The Next Steps in the Democratic Republic of Congo. Draft, Consulting Assistance on Economic Reform / Harvard Institute for International Development, June.
1997b   *The Reconstruction of War-Torn Economies.* Cambridge: Consulting Assistance on Economic Reform / Harvard Institute for International Development

Hay, R., and B. Walker
1996   Sector Investment Programmes in Africa: An Evaluation. Case Study:
       Mozambique Health Sector Recovery Programme. Unpublished report.
Holdstock, D.
1996   Peace through health. *Medicine, Conflict and Survival* 12: 281.
Holtzman, S.
1999   *Rethinking 'Relief' and 'Development' in Transition from Conflict.* Washington, DC:
       The Brookings Institution Project on Internal Displacement.
Hope, K.
1999   Kosovo: Rebuilding getting underway, *Europe* (November) 391.
International Monetary Fund and World Bank
2001   *Assistance to Post-Conflict Countries and the HIPC Framework.* Washington DC:
       World Bank.
Johnson, C.
2002   The strategic framework review: Lessons for post-Taliban Afghanistan. *HPN
       Newsletter Humanitarian Exchange Issue 20.* Available online at: <http://
       www.odihpn.org/report.asp?reportID=2418>.
Kibreab, G.
2000   When refugees come home: the relationship between stayees and returnees in
       post-conflict Eritrea. *Journal of Contemporary Africa Studies* 20(1): 53–80.
Kloos, H.
1998   Primary health care in Ethiopia under three political systems: Community
       participation in a war torn society. *Social Science and Medicine* 46 (4-5): 505–522.
Kreimer, A., J. Eriksson, M. Arnold, and C. Scott
1998   *The World Bank's Experience with Post-Conflict Reconstruction.* Operations
       Evaluation Department. Available online at: <http://lnweb18.worldbank.org/oed/
       oeddoclib.nsf/b57456d58aba40e585256ad400736404/f753e43e728a27b38525
       681700503796/$FILE/PostCon.pdf>.
Kreimer, A., R. Muscat, A. Elwan, and M. Arnold
2000   Bosnia and Herzegovina: Post-Conflict Reconstruction. Washington, DC: World
       Bank.
Kumar, K.
1997   *Rebuilding Societies after Civil War: Critical Roles for International Assistance.*
       Boulder, CO: Lyne Rienner.
Lake, A., ed.
1990   *After the Wars: Reconstruction in Afghanistan, Indochina, Central America, Southern
       Africa and the Horn of Africa.* New Brunswick, NJ: Transaction Books.
Lanjouw, S., J. Macrae, and A. Zwi
1999   Rehabilitating health services in Cambodia: the challenge of coordination in
       chronic political emergencies. *Health Policy and Planning.* 14 (3): 229–242.
Lederach, J.P.
1997   *Building Peace: Sustainable Reconciliation in Divided Societies.* Washington DC:
       United States Institute of Peace Press.

Lisenmeyer, W.
1989   Foreign nations, international organizations, and their impact on health conditions in Nicaragua since 1979. *International Journal of Health Services* 19: 509–529.

Loretti, A., X. Leus, and B. Van Holsteijn
2001   Relevant in times of turmoil: WHO and public health in unstable situations. *Prehospital Disaster Medicine* 16(4): 184–191.

Macrae, J.
1995   *Dilemmas of 'Post'-conflict Transition: Lessons from the Health Sector.* ODI Network Paper 12. Available online at: <www.odi.org>.
1997   Dilemmas of legitimacy, sustainability and coherence: rehabilitating the health sector. In K. Kumar (ed.), *Rebuilding Societies after Civil War—Critical Roles for International Assistance.* London: Lynne Reinner.

Macrae, J., M. Bradbury, and S. Jaspars, D. Jonson, and M. Duffield
1997   Conflict, the continuum and chronic emergencies: A critical analysis of the scope for linking relief, rehabilitation and development planning in Sudan. *Disasters.* Set 21 (3): 223–243.

Macrae, J., A. Zwi, and H. Birungi
1995   *A Healthy Peace?: Rehabilitation & Development of The Health Sector In a Post-Conflict Situation—The Case of Uganda.* London: London School of Hygiene and Tropical Medicine.

Macrae, J., A. Zwi, and V. Forsythe
1995a   Aid policy in transition: A preliminary analysis of 'post'-conflict rehabilitation of the health sector. *Journal of International Development* 7(4): 669–684.
1995b   *Post-Conflict Rehabilitation: Preliminary Issues For Consideration By The Health Sector.* Conflict and Health Series No. 2. London: London School of Hygiene and Tropical Medicine.

Macrae, J., A. Zwi, and L. Gilson
1996   A triple burden for health sector reform: "Post-conflict" rehabilitation in Uganda. *Social Science and Medicine* 42 (7): 1095–1108.

MacQueen, G., and J. Santa-Barbara
2000   Peace building through health initiatives. *British Medical Journal* 321: 293–296.

Maneti, A.
2002   *Public health in post-conflict: Lessons learnt from the FYR Macedonia. Health in Emergencies.* Issue No. 13. Geneva: World Health Organization. Available online at: <http://www.who.int/disasters/tg.cfm?doctypeID=30>.

Milas, S., and J. Latif
2000   The political economy of complex emergency and recovery in northern Ethiopia. *Disasters* (4): 363–379.

Moore, D.
2001   Humanitarian agendas, state reconstruction and democratisation processes in war-torn societies. New Issues in Refugee Research Working Paper No. 24. University of Natal, South Africa.

Morris, K.
2001   Growing pains of East Timor: Health of an infant nation. *Lancet* 357: 873–877.

Murray, C., G. King, A. Lopez, N. Tomijima, and E. Krug
  2002 Armed conflict as a public health problem. *British Medical Journal* 324: 346–349.
Muscat, R.
  1995 *Conflict and Reconstruction: Roles for the World Bank.* Washington, DC: World Bank.
Muslow, B.
  1998 Angola: The search for peace and reconstruction. Pp. 179–207 in O. Furley and R. May, eds. *Peacekeeping in Africa.* Aldershot, UK: Ashgate Publishing.
Nat, J.C., M. Cullen, and J. Mendelson Forman
  1998 *Conflict Prevention and Post-Conflict Reconstruction: Perspectives and Prospects.* Workshop Report, World Bank, August. Available online at: <http://wbln0018. worldbank.org/Networks/ESSD/icdb.nsf/D4856F112E805DF4852566C9007C 27A6/B86BCB448F0C5E9E85256849007831ED/$FILE/ParisReport.pdf>.
Noormahomed, A.R., and M. Segall
  1992 *The Public Health Sector in Mozambique: A Post-War Strategy for Rehabilitation and Sustained Development.* (English version printed by WHO in 1993, original version printed in Portugal).
Obidegwu, C.
  1999 *Rwanda: Policies for Post-Conflict Socio-Economic Change.* Washington, DC: World Bank
Okounzi, S.A., and J. Macrae
  1995 Whose policy is it anyway? International and national influences on health policy development in Uganda. *Health Policy and Planning* 10(2): 122–132.
Ospina, S., and Hohe, T.
  2002 *Traditional Power Structures and Local Governance in East Timor: A Case Study of the Community Empowerment Project.* Geneva: Graduate Institute of Development Studies.
Patrick, I.
  2001 East Timor emerging from conflict: the role of local NGOs and international assistance. *Disasters.* 25(1): 48–66.
Patrick, S.
  1998 *The Check is in the Mail: Improving the Delivery and Co-ordination of Post-conflict Assistance.* New York: Center on International Studies. Available online at: <http://www.reliefweb.int/w/rwb.nsf/WCE?OpenForm>.
Patrick, S., and S. Forman
  2000 *Intentions: Pledges of Aid for Postconflict Recovery.* Boulder, CO: Lynne Rienner.
Pavignani, E., and M. Beesley
  1999 *Working Against the Odds: Institutional Support in the Angolan Health Sector.* A presentation at the London School of Hygiene and Tropical Medicine.
Pavignani, E., and A. Colombo
  2001 *Providing Health Services in Countries Disrupted by Civil Wars: A Comparative Analysis of Mozambique and Angola. 1975–2000.* Available online at: <http://www.who. int/disastesr/hpb/case_studies/mozang.html.>.
Pavignani, E., and J.R. Durao
  1999 Managing external resources in Mozambique: building new relationships on shifting sands? *Health Policy and Planning.* 14(3): 243–253.

Pedersen, J., and Arneberg, M., eds.
    1999   *Social and Economic Conditions in East Timor.* New York and Oslo: Columbia University and Fafo Institute of Applied Social Science.
Pekmez, J.
    2000   *The Intervention by the International Community and the Rehabilitation of Kosovo.* Geneva: Centre for Applied Studies in International Negotiation.
Peters, D.
    1997   Emergency Recovery and Reintegration Program: World Bank Rapid Health Sector Assessment (draft). Unpublished.
Planning and Research Centre
    1994   *The National Health Plan for the Palestinian People: Objectives and Strategies.* Jerusalem: Planning and Research Centre.
Pugh, M.
    1998   *Post-Conflict Rehabilitation: Social and Civil Dimensions.* Geneva: Centre for Applied Studies in International Negotiation.
Pugh, M., ed.
    2000a *Post-Conflict Regeneration.* Basingstoke, UK: Macmillan.
    2000b *Regeneration of War-Torn Societies. Global Issues.* London: Macmillan.
Robson, P., ed.
    2001   *Communities and Reconstruction in Angola.* Guelph, Canada: Development Workshop.
Sharp, T., F. Burkle, A. Vaughn, R. Chotani, and R.J. Brennan
    2002   Challenges and opportunities for humanitarian relief in Afghanistan. *Clinical Infectious Diseases* 15(34) Suppl 5: S215–228.
Shuey, D., F. Qosaj, E. Schouten, and A. Zwi
    2002   Planning for health sector reform in post-conflict situations: Kosovo 1999–2000. *Health Policy.*
Simpson, G.
    1997   Reconstruction and reconciliation: Emerging from transition by Graeme Simpson. *Development in Practice* 7(4): 475–478.
Sondorp, E., T. Kaiser, and A. Zwi
    2001   Beyond emergency care: challenges to health planning in complex emergencies. *Tropical Medicine and International Health* 6(12): 965–970.
Sorensen, B.
    1997   *Women and Post-Conflict Reconstruction.* Occasional Paper No. 3 Geneva: War-Torn Societies Project, United Nations Research Institute for Social Development.
Stewart, F., and F.P. Humphreys
    1997   Civil conflict in developing countries over the last quarter century: an empirical overview of the economic and social consequences. *Oxford Development Studies* 35: 11–42.
Stiefel, M.
    1999   *Rebuilding after War: Lessons from the War-Torn Societies Project.* Geneva: United Nations Research Institute for Social Development/Professional Society of International Studies.

Tishkov, V.

2001   *Understanding Violence for Post-Conflict Reconstruction in Chechnya*, Geneva: Centre for Applied Studies in International Negotiation.

Thompson, M.

1997   Conflict, reconstruction and reconciliation: Reciprocal lessons for NGOs in Southern Africa and Central America. *Development in Practice 7*(4): 505–509.

Toole, M.

1997   Complex emergencies: refugee and other populations. Pp. 419–442 in E. Noji, ed., *The Public Health Consequences of Disasters*. Oxford: Oxford University Press.

Tulloch, J.

2002   *Health Sector Reconstruction in East Timor*. Health in Emergencies. Issue No. 13. Geneva: World Health Organization. Available online at: <http://www.who.int/disasters/tg.cfm? doctypeID=30>.

Tvedten, I.

1997   *Angola. Struggle for Peace and Reconstruction*. Boulder, CO: Westview Press.

Ugalde, A., P. Richards, and A. Zwi

1999   Health consequences of war and political violence. *Encyclopaedia of violence, peace and conflict* 2: 103–121.

Ugalde, A., E. Selva-Sutter, C. Castillo, C. Paz, S. Canas, and A. Zwi

2000   The health costs of war: can they be measured? Lessons from El Salvador. *British Medical Journal 321*: 169–172.

United Nations

1996   *An Inventory of Post-Conflict Peace-Building Activities*. New York: United Nations.

United Nations Civil Administration Health and Social Services

1999   *Interim Health Policy Guidelines for Kosovo and Six Month Action Plan*. Pristina.

United Nations Institute for Namibia

1986   *Namibia: Perspectives for National Reconstruction and Development*. Lusaka: United Nations Institute for Namibia.

U.S. Agency for International Development

1997   Operational Challenges in Post-Conflict Societies, U.S. Agency for International Development Workshop, Washington DC, October 28–29.

Vass, A.

2001   Peace through health: this new movement needs evidence, not just ideology. *British Medical Journal 323*: 1020.

Weiss Fagen, P.

1995   *After the Conflict: a Review of Selected Sources on Rebuilding War-torn Societies*. Geneva: United Nations Research Institute for Social Development, Programme for International Security Studies.

Wood, B.D.

2000   Reconstruction: A daunting task. *Europe* (July/August) no. 398.

World Bank

1994   *Cambodia: From Rehabilitation to Reconstruction*. Washington, DC: World Bank.

1995a *Cambodia Rehabilitation Program: Implementation and Outlook*. February, Washington, DC: World Bank.

1995b Staff Appraisal Report—Republic of Mozambique—Health Sector Recovery Project. Unpublished report. Washington, DC: World Bank.

1996a Bosnia and Herzegovina: Priority Reconstruction Projects Update, June. Washington, DC: World Bank.

1996b *Bosnia and Herzegovina: The Priority Reconstruction Program—Sectoral Projects and Programs, as of July 31.* Washington, DC: World Bank.

1996c *Bosnia and Herzegovina: Toward Economic Recovery.* Washington, DC: World Bank.

1996d *Cambodia: From Recovery to Sustained Development.* Washington, DC: World Bank.

1997 *A Framework for World Bank Involvement in Post-Conflict Reconstruction.* April 25. Washington, DC: World Bank.

1998a *Post-Conflict Reconstruction.* Precis Report No. 169. Available online at: <http://wbln0018.worldbank.org/oed/oeddoclib.nsf/3b01efb621e6553785256885007d98b9/9a6f0021ceff9e89852567f5005d9176/$FILE/169precis.pdf>.

1998b *Post-Conflict Reconstruction: The Role of the World Bank.* Washington, DC: World Bank.

1998c *Post-Conflict Reconstruction: The Role of the World Bank. Environmentally and Socially Sustainable Development Network.* Washington, DC: World Bank.

1998d *The World Bank's Experience with Post-Conflict Reconstruction.* Washignton, DC: World Bank Operations Evaluation Department.

1999 *East Timor Joint Assessment Mission Background Report.* December. Available online at: <http://wbln0018.worldbank.org/eap/eap.nsf/6ab4a442217f81de852567c9006b5ef9/a67abe6406537dcb85256847007dff36?OpenDocument.>

2000 *Post-Conflict Reconstruction, Country Case Study Series.* Washington, DC: World Bank.

World Bank, European Commission and European Bank for Reconstruction and Development

1996a Bosnia and Herzegovina: The Priority Reconstruction and Recovery Program: The Challenges Ahead, Discussion Paper No. 2, April. Washington, DC: World Bank.

1996b Bosnia and Herzegovina: Towards Economic Recovery, Discussion Paper No. 1, April. Washington, DC: World Bank.

Zwi, A., A. Ugalde, and P. Richards

1999 Impact of war and political violence on health services. *Encyclopaedia of Violence, Peace and Conflict* 1: 679–690.

Zwi, A., A. Ugalde, E. Pavignani, and S. Fustukian

In   Challenge, opportunity and danger: reconstructing health sectors after significant
press periods of conflict.

Appendix
D

About the Authors

Jim Tulloch has worked in international public health for the past 27 years as a clinician, researcher, technical consultant, and administrator. He has worked on control of smallpox, diarrhea, and acute respiratory diseases and on malaria research. From 1992 he oversaw the development by the World Health Organization (WHO) of the strategy of integrated management of childhood illness. He was director of child and adolescent health and development at WHO headquarters before being seconded to the United Nations Transitional Administration in East Timor, where he led the UN health sector team working with East Timorese counterparts to rebuild the health system during 2000 and 2001. He is currently WHO representative and team leader in Cambodia. He has a bachelor of medicine/bachelor of surgery (MBBS) degree from the University of Adelaide, Australia.

Fadia Saadah is currently the sector manager for health, nutrition, and population for the East Asia and Pacific Region at the World Bank. She has worked in the areas of health policy and strategies, health system reforms, and maternal and child health programs, as well as nutrition. She was the task team leader for the initial effort of reconstruction and development of the health sector in East Timor that resulted in the first health sector program. She has a PhD in population studies and a master's degree in biostatistics from Johns Hopkins University. She also has a master's degree in epidemiology from the American University of Beirut, Lebanon, where she worked before coming to the United States.

55

Rui Maria de Araujo was a house surgeon at Dili Referral Hospital, East Timor, from 1994 to 1998. During the transition of his country to independence, he was head of the Policy and Planning Section of the Division of Health Services in the First Transitional Government of East Timor. In June 2001 he became head of the Division of Health Services, and in September 2001 he was sworn in as the first minister for health in the Second Transitional Government. Since May 2002 he has been the minister for health of the First Constitutional Government of the Democratic Republic of Timor-Leste. He has an MD from Udayana Medical School, Bali, Indonesia and an MPH from Otago University, Dunedin, New Zealand.

Rui Paulo de Jesus worked as a district medical officer and as a general practitioner before the crisis of late 1999. He served as a member of the Interim Health Authority from its creation in February 2000. He was head of the Health Services Delivery Section of the Division of Health Services in the First Transitional Government of East Timor. He was also an Expanded Programme of Immunisation (EPI) program consultant for UNICEF in Dili, East Timor. He acted as director general of health until 2002, when he left to pursue a master's degree in public health and epidemiology at the University of Hawaii. He has an MD from the Faculty of Medicine, Udayana University, Denpasar, Bali, Indonesia.

Sergio Lobo is a surgeon, and in 2000 he was the only East Timorese with a clinical specialist qualification. He returned to his country in late 1999 and was instrumental in setting up the East Timor Health Professionals Working Group, which he chaired. As coordinator of the Interim Health Authority from its creation in February 2000, he played a key role throughout the first year of the reconstruction of the health system.

Isabel Hemming has had over 15 years experience in providing technical and management assistance internationally, in both post-conflict and development situations. She has worked with NGOs, international organizations, UN agencies (including UNICEF and WHO), donors, and the World Bank. Her work in the past five years has focused on support and assistance to ministries of health in Tajikistan, East Timor, and Afghanistan, primarily in the areas of health policy, planning, and reform. Other countries in which she has worked include Azerbaijan, Iraq, Pakistan, Somalia, and Sudan. She has a PhD in anthropology from UCLA.

Janet Nassim is a senior operations officer, health, nutrition and population at the World Bank. She was a member of the Joint Donor Mission that prepared the first Trust Fund for East Timor-supported Health Sector Rehabilitation and Development project, and has been involved ever since. In addition to working in Timor Leste, she has worked in countries of the Middle East. Trained as a demographer, she has worked at the World Bank since 1987, with a focus on population and reproductive health, an area in which she has written several publications. Ms. Nassim has degrees in sociology from London University, in social work from Birmingham University, and in demography from Georgetown University, Washington, D.C.

Ian Morris is a senior human resource specialist in the East Asia Human Development Unit of the World Bank and is now based in the Bank's Sydney office, where he is responsible for coordinating health, education, and social protection programs for the World Bank in East Timor, Papua New Guinea, and the Pacific Islands. Since October 2000, he has led the World Bank team and joint donor review missions that have supervised the first Health Sector Rehabilitation Project and prepared and supervised the second project. He has extensive experience with the World Bank working on social sector programs in Pakistan, Nepal, and the Pacific Islands and in December 2001 led the international team responsible for the initial needs assessment for the health sector in Afghanistan. Prior to joining the World Bank, he worked as a development consultant in South and East Asia for 8 years and for the government of Papua New Guinea for 10 years. He has an honors degree in economics from La Trobe University, Melbourne, Australia.

OTHER PUBLICATIONS OF THE ROUNDTABLE ON THE DEMOGRAPHY OF FORCED MIGRATION